# Oxygenation is the Solution

# Deaths from Covid-19 and Global Legal Insights for Medical Practice

## An Insider's Perspective

Brian Lynch LLB., Solicitor

ISBN: 978-1-7391012-4-4

Published by Book Hub Publishing.
An Independent Publishing House with Offices in Galway and Limerick, Ireland.

The Book Hub Publishing Group is committed to inclusion and diversity. We print all our books on forestry sustainable paper.

# Table of Contents

# Dedication

*To my loving mother, Mona Lynch (1919-2015), a widow at the age of 40, a mother of nine boys and one girl and for her decision to be a warrior and not a victim.*

# Testimonials

'This publication will give readers food for thought about hyperbaric oxygen therapy as a potential treatment from both a medical and legal perspective. Importantly, the author explores concepts of informed consent from several jurisdictions and draws on some relevant case law. It is a publication that challenges much of what is regarded as the norm in healthcare and ethics and medical negligence including the concept of controlled clinical trials. The author is unique in that he has considerable personal experience of hyperbaric oxygen treatment and is a provider of such services and a practicing lawyer. Such matters are declared.

This book will be of interest to the public, patients, policy makers and legal and medical practitioners and will stimulate debate. Without doubt, independent systematic reviews of hyperbaric oxygen therapy are needed as are measured consideration by policy makers. The author is to be congratulated for tackling such contentious issues in his forthright style and for his advocacy. All such matters have been sharpened by the Covid-19 pandemic and the book describes some experience of such advocacy during the pandemic. Such matters are topical and controversial.'

—Mr SIMON P KELLY FRCSEd, FRCOphth, FEBO, DHC (Hon)
Consultant Ophthalmologist
Beaumont Hospital
Bolton
BL6 4LA
England

‘In the increasingly regulated and questioning era we now live in this is a timely publication which will be of valuable assistance and guidance to many; particularly Lawyers, Coroners and Medical Doctors.

Coroners’ enquiries and the inquests they hold are not confined to simply establishing the medical cause of death. The role of the Coroner has been expanded by the Coroners Amendment Act 2019 and as interpreted in a number of important decisions of the Superior Courts in Ireland over the past seven decades.

Doctors, Lawyers, Coroners, members of An Garda Siochana, The HSE, Politicians and Civil Servants will benefit from reading this book.’

—Patrick O’Connor, LLB-Coroner for the District of Mayo.

---

‘This is a powerful book. Brian Lynch, an Irish lawyer with an insider’s knowledge of hyperbaric oxygenation tells a true story about how in different parts of the globe, medical practice managed or mismanaged patients with COVID-19 and post COVID-19 conditions. It’s an essential read for both medical professionals and US army veterans who have Post Traumatic Stress Disorder, Traumatic Brain Injury or are suicidal who are seeking State and Federal support for paying for hyperbaric oxygenation.

The story could equally be about supporting TreatNow veterans. This gripping story explains the law that governs what a patient must be told prior to any medical intervention. Brian’s readable style challenges medical research methods and clinical practice guidelines to do with decision making surrounding healthcare.’

—Rob Beckman, www.treatnow.org
A Citizen Response to the Suicide and Concussion Crises.

# Acknowledgements

This is an amazingly complex science involving genes and cell proliferation using oxygenation under pressure.

Nonetheless, what's simple is that oxygenation under pressure is a treatment for injured tissue no matter what the cause, and it works on injured tissue in any location of the body, and is especially valuable in the brain.

I acknowledge the leaders in the hyperbaric oxygenation medical community who carried out research and influenced others by writing about their clinical experiences. This influenced patients as decision-makers to use this treatment option and, using scientific evidence, proved to the wider medical community the powerful benefits of it.

Dr Orval Cunningham (1880-1937) in Cleveland, Ohio, famously used regular bellows to put pressure inside air-filled pressure cabins. Dr Cunningham is of special value to lawyers because he was wrongly condemned in an unscientific fashion by the consensus opinion within the leadership at the Medical Association at the time.

The medical community can now prove this was unjustified criticism, resulting in patients suffering from disease or dying unnecessarily.

The point is also of legal value because Dr Cunningham has been proven right by advances in modern forms of scientific measurements and continued clinical experiences.

Dr Cunningham understood the influence of changing atmospheric pressure and that, when pressure decreased at altitudes in the mountains, it was detrimental to the oxygenation of blood and tissue.

This led him to see how pressure artificially created in the pressure cabins on the whole body had the reverse effect of the decreased pressure at altitudes.

In 1931, the Nobel Prize for Physiology and Medicine was awarded to Dr Otto Warburg (1883-1970) for his investigations into the metabolism of tumours and the respiration of cells, particularly cancer cells.

In 2019, the Nobel Prize in Physiology and Medicine was awarded to three scientists who, according to the Nobel Prize committee, 'established the basis for our understanding of how oxygen levels affect cellular metabolism and physiological function.

Their discoveries have also paved the way for promising new strategies to fight anaemia, cancer and many other diseases'.

I acknowledge the work of Dr Richard Neubauer (1924–2007), who since the 1970s had been reporting his wide clinical experiences on successful outcomes for neurological dysfunction. Dr Neubauer appeared on television many times and has published several books, articles and papers.

Dr L Bojić in Croatia reported on a case series study on hyperbaric oxygenation for glaucoma in 1993. What is of value is that, as a result, the national and private health insurance agreed to pay for hyperbaric oxygenation for treating glaucoma.[1]

Dr Jasna Pavičić Astaloš, a Consultant Ophthalmologist trained in Croatia who works in Ireland, has been one of the forerunners in promoting hyperbaric oxygenation for eye disease.

There is universal gratitude from patients for Dr Pierre Thirion, a Consultant Radiation Oncologist who trained in France and works in Dublin, as he has brought about a dramatic change to quality of life for people that is for the better. His great achievement is the

---

1 Bojić L et al., 'Hyperbaric oxygen dose of choice in the treatment of glaucoma', Arh Hig Rada Toksikol, (1993), pp. 239-47. Available online at: https://pubmed.ncbi.nlm.nih.gov/8311697/

example that he persuaded his hospital and, subsequently, the Irish Health Service Executive to pay for private hyperbaric oxygenation for radiation oncology injury as standard care.

In his lifelong work, Dr Paul Harch MD inspired so many doctors to inform people about hyperbaric oxygenation for neurological disorders. Dr Harch worked with Dr Edward Fogarty, a radiologist, who is opening people's eyes with the use of PET images before and after treatments by showing the improvements in the brain for people with Alzheimer's disease. Dr Paul Harch is the co-author of *The Oxygen Revolution*, which is a valuable read. Dr Harch is a Clinical Professor and the Department of Internal Medicine Director at the Medical Centre of Louisiana Hyperbaric Medicine Department. Dr Harch was the first President of the International Hyperbaric Medicine Association. He and his wife, Nurse Juliette Lucarini Harch, both worked with the authors of the first studies from China on COVID-19 so the rest of the world would know clinically about the uses of hyperbaric oxygenation for COVID-19.

Nurse Marcus Speyrer and Dr Kerry Thibodeaux, the first American nurse and doctor who wrote a case report on the successful use of hyperbaric oxygenation for COVID-19, also partook in a video conference to be sent to the Irish Parliamentary Response Committee to the COVID-19 Pandemic on the use of hyperbaric oxygenation.

In separate studies, both Dr Parambir Dulai of the University of California San Diego and Dr M Bekheit in Egypt explain the mechanisms of action of hyperbaric oxygenation in its application for inflammatory bowel disease.

What is of value is that Dr Bekheit explained in the *British Medical Journal* how one single case (n=1) of remission in refractory ulcerative colitis caused hyperbaric oxygenation to be offered to patients in Egypt since 1994.

Dr Shai Efrati is a professor in the Sagol School of Neuroscience, Tel-Aviv University, Israel, and Medical Director of the Sagol Research Centre. Dr Efrati has inspired and promoted a new way of thinking. He uses advances in technology to prove the application of science in the healing of injured hypoxic tissue, whether in the brain, in erectile dysfunction or in other parts of the body. He has said in a way one found easy to understand: 'An injury is an injury no matter where it is or what caused it…'.

On the subject of publicity for the known benefits, I acknowledge Timothy Ferriss, who has been 75 weeks on the New York Times Best Sellers list. Of great interest is an interview podcast he did with Professor Dominic D'Agostino about the ketogenic diet, hyperbaric oxygenation and cancer as an adjunct to standard care.2 While randomised controlled trials are underway in the US, the use of hyperbaric oxygenation as an adjunct to chemotherapy and radiation oncology is standard care in Japan and parts of Europe.

Dr Daniel Amen, an American psychiatrist and author of the *Brain Warrior's Way,* has done over 110,000 SPECT scans of the brain. From looking at SPECT images of the brain, he estimates that 50% of people who seek treatment for mental illness have, in fact, brain tissue injury and not a mental or mind disorder. This is inflammation of the brain. His books and talks are about healing the brain and brain tissue injury by treating inflammation. He proposes a combination of diet change, dietary supplements and hyperbaric oxygenation.

The neurosurgeon, Dr Kewal K Jain (1928-2021) and his co-authors of the *Textbook of Hyperbaric Medicine,* now in its sixth edition since 1989, have completed invaluable work in education.

---

2 Tim Ferris, '#188: Dom D'Agostino on Disease Prevention, Cancer, and Living Longer', The Tim Ferris Show, (2018). Available online at: https://tim.blog/2018/06/06/the-tim-ferriss-show-transcripts-dom-dagostino-on-disease-prevention-cancer-and-living-longer/

Dr Dominic D'Agostino, PhD, is acknowledged as a great scientist and is of great value as an advocate and public speaker. Professor D'Agostino is an Associate Professor in the Department of Molecular Pharmacology and Physiology at the University of South Florida Morsani College of Medicine. The hypothesis is that this treatment may help humans as the Ketogenic Diet and hyperbaric oxygenation prolong survival in mice with systemic metastatic cancer.

I thank both Dr Jacek Kot, the then General Secretary of the European Committee for Hyperbaric Medicine, and Dr Nick Bird, the then President of the Undersea Hyperbaric Medicine Society, for their helpful phone calls and correspondence.

Professor Ruiyong Chen, co-author and lead author of the first two studies on COVID-19 from China, corresponded with me and helped me understand medical ethics regarding the known benefits of hyperbaric oxygenation and the complexities of educating the medical profession.

One of the greatest influencers of our time has been Professor Philip James, the author of *Oxygen and the Brain – The Journey of our Lifetime*. In many phone conversations and exchanges of emails with Professor James, I learned about the complexity of oxygenation and gene therapy and their value in medicine. I would not have completed this task without his inspiration and help.

On food, nutrition and lifestyle, I acknowledge the advice of the cardiologist Dr Aseem Malhotra for metabolic health.

Dr Jason Fung, a Canadian-based nephrologist and Jimmy Moore's work on fasting have improved people's quality of life. I value their book *The Complete Guide to Fasting: Heal Your Body Through Intermittent, Alternate-Day, and Extended Fasting.*

The value of publicity and education is acknowledged as being important. Mr Duane Pohlman, a journalist, reports on television in the US that 'more than a dozen hospitals across the country say hyperbaric oxygen therapy (HBOT) is saving the lives of even the most critically ill coronavirus patients'.3 His reporting resulted in an inaccurate article being removed from the Food and Drug Administration's website, discussed later.

I thank television presenter Ilan Lukatch and researcher Tal Moysa in Israel for their television programme in Hebrew with English subtitles, *Hyperbaric Oxygen Therapy*, on Israel Friday Studio News.4 The programme was about the Sagol Research Centre in Tel Aviv.

To James Badenoch Queen's Counsel, an English barrister who acted for Mrs Montgomery who was not told she could have a caesarean section. He persuaded the UK Supreme Court that earlier UK decisions on the law of informed consent were mistaken.

To Liam Deasy (a Multiple Sclerosis sufferer) who, with other volunteers, set up a non-emergency hyperbaric oxygenation facility in Bandon. It's run by volunteers from the community, in the community for the community.

To all the similar centres run by laypeople in the community in Europe.

To Gareth O'Callaghan, an Irish author and much-loved radio broadcaster who encouraged me to write this book. He came to use OxyGeneration as a client with Multiple System Atrophy (MSA) and wrote a remarkable account of how he found OxyGeneration helpful.

To Niall MacGiolla Bhuí, PhD who inspired me and helped bring this book to publication.

I make a special acknowledgement of the pioneering work of Des Quigley who, as an engineer and enthusiastic diver with his wife Alison, set up in 1996 the National Hyperbaric Centre in Dublin, Ireland.

---

[3] Duane Pohlman, 'New treatment promises hope during pandemic', *Local 12*, (2020). Available online at: https://local12.com/news/investigates/new-treatment-promises-hope-during-pandemic-cincinnati-duane-pohlman-coronavirus-covid

4 'Hyperbaric Oxygen Therapy', Israel Friday Studio News, (2017). Available online with English subtitles at: https://www.youtube.com/watch?v=gLYk9u9o5fQ

# About the Author and His Journey into the Hyperbaric World

The author was born in Galway on 3 May 1955 and was educated at St Ignatius College, Galway, and Mungret College, Limerick. He studied mathematics, psychology, sociology and politics before taking primary and post-primary degrees in law at the National University of Ireland, Galway. Brian qualified as a solicitor in 1980 at the Incorporated Law Society of Ireland in Dublin and practices as a solicitor (lawyer) in Ireland at Brian Lynch and Associates.

As part of this law firm's general practice work, he is involved in various professional negligence laws, including medical negligence. The firm successfully acted for people infected with MRSA due to alleged breaches of statutory duty and negligence in proceedings against private hospitals and Ireland's Health Service Executive.

Following a serious horse-riding accident in 2015 in Warwickshire, UK, the author was taken by a helicopter ambulance to the Coventry and Warwickshire Hospital. He appreciated that his life was saved by the surgical interventions of doctors and allied healthcare professionals on arrival. A few decades earlier, his internal injuries would have taken his life within hours if he did not have the surgery to bypass a severed urethra.

Hyperbaric oxygenation was used to help Brian's rapid recovery from severe trauma, pelvic fracture, pain, internal injuries, a chest infection, fat embolism syndrome (caused by the fractured bone in his blood), stress and various surgeries. He understands that he owes his recovery and quality of life to the medical teams and hyperbaric oxygenation.

After 10 days in the UK hospital, Brian was transferred by air ambulance to the St James's Hospital in Dublin, Ireland, where he had his first session of hyperbaric oxygenation the following day. Using a wheelchair and being transported by wheelchair in a taxi, Brian went from a hospital bed in St James's Hospital to the nearby National Hyperbaric Oxygen Centre in Dublin for daily sessions. He is grateful to the medical community for looking after him and encouraging him, and attributes his first stage of rapid and quality recovery to the help of some 20 sessions of hyperbaric oxygenation, doing five a week for four weeks.

The author was grateful to have reduced his predicted time in a wheelchair from 13 weeks to seven. He was aware that an opioid (narcotic) for pain relief was addictive and understood the importance of cutting time on them. Hyperbaric oxygenation helped by rapidly healing the injured tissue and reducing the painful inflammation. Brian decided to stop taking the painkillers early and found he did not need them.

He later read that doctors routinely prescribe hyperbaric oxygenation before and after surgery, as it speeds healing time based on studies in the UK and Japan. At the time of using the treatments, for the author it was a case of: if it was good enough for John Magnier's million-dollar bloodstock and good enough for well-known sports players for injuries and rapid recovery, it was definitely good enough for him.

It was sufficient information that hyperbaric oxygenation was used in sports medicine, especially in Japan. When the Japanese rugby squad came to the UK in 2015 for the Rugby World Cup, they intentionally located their training camp near a town with a hyperbaric oxygenation facility and used it every day.5

Brian was impressed that hyperbaric oxygenation reduces pain and time on painkillers, or makes it possible to endure without them, or even reduces the dosage of painkillers (although it is not a painkiller itself). The effect relieves pain as it heals the injured tissue and reduces the inflammation causing the pain, as the oxygenation feeds into the cellular hypoxia (severe shortage of oxygen). When he was having his urethra (tube between the bladder and the outside) reconstruction surgery, success and recovery was in the balance and not guaranteed. He was, as one can imagine, happy to try anything to tip the balance in his favour.

Like other patients in his position, he did not want to risk having a permanent catheter, nappies and a urine bag, so hyperbaric oxygenation was used to increase his likelihood of recovery for tissue injury, especially nerve endings. Brian did a further 37 sessions by driving from Galway to Dublin each day. Unfortunately, the National Hyperbaric Medicine Unit at Galway University Hospital could not take him.

Looking back, he feels that listening to other people's powerful stories of recovery using oxygenation inspired him to bring OxyGeneration to Galway.

From his own personal and professional experiences within the field of medicine and medical law, his interest in and understanding of the social value of the law of disclosure of

---

5 Rob Hunt, 'England crash out of Rugby World Cup while Japan use HBOT to get players fighting fit!' in Oxygen Healing, (2015). Available online at: https://oxygenhealing.co.uk/news/england-crash-rugby-world-cup-japan-hbot-players-fighting-fit/

information and informed consent to medical interventions continues to develop and flourish.

These events have brought him to contact doctors and technician professionals with clinical experience in hyperbaric oxygenation. Brian realised this hyperbaric treatment option would become more common if patients were told about the known benefits of hyperbaric oxygenation. This also meant it would be of benefit to more people. As he sees it, what's stopping this is that the law and ethical doctrine of balanced disclosure is not being complied with. Treating someone after obtaining an invalid informed consent prior to any medical intervention is not properly understood by the medical community and hospital management.

The author's experience on this journey firstly led to bringing OxyGeneration to his hometown, Galway. His insider's insight into the medical community enabled him to see solutions to some of the medico-legal problems facing this community and inspired him to write this book.

## Author's Statement of Conflicted Interest

Following my accident and subsequent hyperbaric oxygenation sessions in Dublin, I became a stakeholder in OxyGeneration, a service provider for profit of hyperbaric oxygenation founded in Galway, Ireland, so any increased use of hyperbaric oxygenation could potentially be of commercial advantage to me. While this makes me biased in a legal sense, it equally gives me an insider's experience.

I am personally conflicted in telling this story. My story is from my layperson's view, who happens to be a lawyer with a legal opinion. I am someone with the advantage of an insider's insight into its uses because I used hyperbaric oxygenation for my own recovery following a serious horse-riding accident in 2015, and for my recovery from Long COVID-19 Syndrome in 2021.

Unfortunately, I have had to defend my right to have an opinion on various medical and scientific issues by stating that one does not have to be a medical doctor to be a patient.

# Preface

This book is a lesson learned from a community of patients and doctors with experience of the scientific basis for the uses of hyperbaric oxygenation and nutritional options as part of their own recovery. I had positive experiences while undergoing my 57 hyperbaric oxygenation sessions at the National Hyperbaric Centre in Dublin. As a result of opening OxyGeneration, a hyperbaric oxygenation facility in Galway, and conversing on an almost daily basis with clients, my experience of the shortcoming of the clinical practice guidelines used by the medical community made me feel compelled to write this book.

If this book becomes part of the medical community's toolkit for clinical practice, the benefits are infinite. As a 'tool' for informed consent, this book can greatly help doctors assist clients in making medical decisions. This, in turn, will put an end to what I and many clinicians see as unnecessary surgical and medical interventions, such as heart surgery, brain surgery, limb amputation, intestine surgery and/or bowel operations to name a few.

Notwithstanding that non-invasive and more patient-friendly options have superseded interventions, the core question posed in this book is: If these interventions are redundant, are they unlawful?

This book is an invaluable pathway for rapid change in medical practice because respectable clinicians need not fear being branded as quacks or risk-takers. Patients must be the only decision-makers on treatment options and take the risks involved. This book does not aim to be a textbook or reference book on the law of informed consent or medical ethics.

Nonetheless, references to medical research, the Medical Council's ethical guidelines and case law are included because they are tools to help a medical professional understand the benefit of hyperbaric oxygenation and the law of informed consent. Values shared are for the benefit of both healthcare professionals and their clients in making decisions about their treatment plans.

This book is a tool to help clinicians see the value of the law of informed consent. Because it's the patient who decides, the clinicians will realise that they are not obliged to only carry out what are redundant but, nonetheless, standard recommended interventions. Again, because it's the patient who decides, the medical community cannot, therefore, criticise one another because of a treatment that the patient chose. Medical professionals don't have to consider themselves under ethical and legal constraint to be carrying out the clinical practice guidelines' standard of care options. Nonetheless, they don't have to carry out unnecessary heart, brain, plastic, orthopaedic, eye or urological surgery, amputations or removal of people's intestines or rectums because it's evidence-based medicine. Similarly, they don't have to recommend and prescribe unnecessary medication just because it's currently perceived to be 'standard care'.

# Chapter One:

# Success with Hyperbaric Oxygenation for COVID-19: A Global Perspective

This story aims to start a conversation that will help the medical community. Dramatic and rapid recoveries of all critically ill patients with COVID-19 came about on 13 April 2020 in the small French city of Opelousas in Louisiana, US. A nurse who worked in a hospital was infected and became critically ill.[6] This nurse and others made their recovery as a result of being given hyperbaric (high pressure) oxygenation in a single-person pressure chamber. This account of events will surprise many, however it's also likely to shock and cause anger because this treatment option was a lost opportunity, as is shown by the global COVID-19 death count of over six million by March 2022.

What is dangerous and, as I see it, problematic from the position of a lawyer defending the professionals treating COVID-

---

[6] Kailey McCarthy, 'Louisiana hospital using Hyperbaric Oxygen Therapy to treat extreme cases of COVID-19,' from *KALB*, (April 2022). Available online at: https://www.kalb.com/content/news/Louisiana-hospital-using-Hyperbaric-Oxygen-Therapy-to-treat-extreme-cases-of-COVID-19-569868541.html

The story about the nurse was told to me personally on the phone by a nurse working in the hospital (Nurse Marcus Speyrer and co-author of the clinical case report).

19 hospitalised patients is that leaders in hyperbaric medicine in the US, South America, Europe and Asia knew about these dramatic recoveries. For this reason, taking reasonable care to know about this treatment option was not the problem. One will see that the problem was a lack of true understanding of the medical law on disclosure that led to the unfortunate events in this story.

The immediate legal puzzle for a fact finder, such as a judge or a jury, is to determine whether a reasonable person in the patient's position, who is critically ill with COVID-19, would have considered this information significant and acted on it. Unfortunately, if the answer is yes, then a fact finder must logically conclude that people died unnecessarily. All this is not complex to explain in layperson's terms or in terms that a person in the patient's position would understand. The point is that a layperson can understand that the hypoxemia (oxygen shortage in the blood), hypoxia tissue injury at a cellular level (oxygen debt in cells) and inflammation caused by COVID-19 can be rapidly reversed by hyperbaric oxygenation. This was a treatment that could have been upscaled by temporarily making use of commercial jet aircraft as hyperbaric oxygenation chambers.

One is sorry to say that this story opens a can of worms nevertheless, an open conversation is needed for the benefit of all involved. However, it's also a story of how the COVID-19 pandemic could have been managed differently. When the events are understood, one is likely to conclude that the medical community did not comply with current medical laws and did not see that they need to change how decisions on treatment options are made. We are all resolute that the same decisions, delays and loss of life are not repeated.

The nurse in this story was at work one day, became too ill to go home and had to be admitted to the hospital as a critically ill patient. This nurse was one of five patients in a study who were seriously or critically ill and opted for hyperbaric oxygenation rather than invasive mechanical ventilation. None in the study succumbed to COVID-19 and they all survived. The patients consented to be part of the first study in the US on the use of hyperbaric oxygenation.

It was added to their care on what Americans call 'compassionate grounds', as hyperbaric oxygenation was not approved by the Food and Drug Administration for treating COVID-19 patients. To be clear, if a treatment option is not Food and Drug Administration approved, doctors are *not* prevented by regulation from recommending it.

On the contrary, one will learn in this book why doctors would be legally and ethically obliged to inform patients about the known benefits of hyperbaric oxygenation as a treatment option as part of balanced disclosure required prior to any medical intervention. In default there is an invalid informed consent and an unethical and unlawful assault and battery on the patient.

In this French city of Opelousas in Louisiana, like in all hospitals around the world, it was a new challenge for those coping with COVID-19. When one becomes critically ill, the level of oxygen saturation becomes dangerously low. From other reported cases, the doctors knew that this meant possible life-threatening pulmonary and cardiac complications.

There were concerns as it was also reported that there was a high death rate of between 50-80% for invasive ventilator-dependent patients however, these figures improved in time.[7] In layperson's terms, the invasive ventilator delivery of oxygen was not enough dosage and patients died. Some 28,319 people had already died of COVID-19 in the US and 884 had died in Louisiana up to the date 13 April 2020, which was the date the first patient (n=1) in Louisiana was given hyperbaric oxygenation. I should point out that the hospital responded to the emergency in the pandemic with commendable speed by assembling the scientific data and publishing a medical report on 1 May 2020.

Nonetheless, medical staff in this hospital were familiar with using hyperbaric oxygenation in the hospital's Wound Treatment Center.

To understand why hyperbaric oxygenation was underused, my story in this chapter is laid out to help healthcare professionals. There is a need to be aware of a legal duty to take reasonable care to explain to a layperson (a patient) about all the reasonable treatment options.

As a lawyer with experience using hyperbaric oxygenation, this has given me a special insider's insight into the legal solutions for medical professionals. This medical law was developed from experiences in law cases from the past, but unfortunately has been overlooked and not universally applied. Globally and largely, although not exclusively, what caused the underuse was calls for experimental randomised controlled trials or other trials before informing patients and politicians of the *already known* benefits.

What's legally problematic is that experiments on humans cannot take place as the scientists and/or doctors by law must

---

[7] Feldmeier, J.J., Kirby, J.P., Buckey, J.C., et al., 'Physiologic and biochemical rationale for treating COVID-19 patients with hyperbaric oxygen', *Undersea & Hyperbaric Medicine*, Vol. 48, No.1, (2021), pp.1-12. Available online at: https://www.uhms.org/images/MiscDocs/Physiologic_and_biochemical_rationale_for_treating_UHM_48-1.pdf

give sufficient information to enable the patient to make an enlightened decision. This has been the position worldwide due to the Nuremberg Code being firmly embedded globally in different forms into nations laws and ethics following World War II.[8] Strictly, it's not an international binding agreement between nations, however, the Nuremberg Code is the accepted standard. It's useful nonetheless to refer to the Nuremberg Code as the global standard because of the important influence it has had.

In layperson's terms, one will tell the narrative of how the known benefits of a treatment used for non-healing wounds became a treatment of choice by COVID-19 patients.

While hyperbaric oxygenation is a complex science, it's not too complex to explain its known benefits for treating COVID-19. Again, in layperson's terms, the coronavirus attacked the body in a way that resulted in an overreaction of the immune system, causing too much inflammation, a shortage of oxygen at tissue level, hypoxia tissue injury at cellular level, tissue dysfunction and even tissue death.

To give some powerful insight about unnecessary loss of life, hyperbaric oxygenation is considered mainstream healthcare. Nevertheless, not all hospitals have hyperbaric chambers, which was part of the ethical and legal problem for treating doctors during the pandemic. It's nonetheless mainstream as public and private healthcare insurance pays for it, however, controversially in the US, insurance does not cover scientific-based applications such as reversing hypoxia, and only pays for a list of named

---

[8] CIRP, 'The Nuremberg Code (1947)', *British Medical Journal*, Vol. 313, No. 7070, (7 December 1996), p. 1448. Quote: 'The judgment by the war crimes tribunal at Nuremberg laid down 10 standards to which physicians must conform when carrying out experiments on human subjects in a new code that is now accepted worldwide.' Available online at: https://media.tghn.org/medialibrary/2011/04/BMJ_No_7070_Volume_313_The_Nuremberg_Code.pdf

medical conditions.[9] Understanding this distinction is key as it's a deciding factor in avoiding the problem in the future.

For insurance cover in the US, medical conditions or diseases must be approved by the Food and Drug Administration. Certain non-healing wounds are covered. From a scientific perspective, the biological phenomena or problem caused by shortage of oxygen at tissue level is addressed by using hyperbaric oxygenation.

A person enters a sealed chamber that is pressurised. While breathing oxygen, the amount of oxygen that dissolves into the blood and tissue is greatly increased in proportion to the pressure. The relevant scientific explanation of how and why it works is summarised here in a few paragraphs. This healing process is widely used in almost every country as a concurrent treatment to prevent limb amputations for people with foot ulcers.[10] [11] On a scientific basis, the determining criteria in an

---

[9] From the Food and Drug Administration website: "As of July 2021, the FDA has cleared hyperbaric chambers for the following disorders: Air and gas bubbles in blood vessels, Anemia (severe anemia when blood transfusions cannot be used), Burns (severe and large burns treated at a specialized burn center), Carbon monoxide poisoning, Crush injury, Decompression sickness (diving risk), Gas gangrene, Hearing loss (complete hearing loss that occurs suddenly and without any known cause), Infection of the skin and bone (severe), Radiation injury, Skin graft flap at risk of tissue death, Vision loss (when sudden and painless in one eye due to blockage of blood flow), Wounds (non-healing, diabetic foot ulcers)" . Available online at: https://www.fda.gov/consumers/consumer-updates/hyperbaric-oxygen-therapy-get-facts

[10] Abidia, A., Laden, G., Kuhan, G., Johnson, B.F., Wilkinson, A.R., Renwick, P.M., Masson, E.A. and McCollum, P.T., 'The role of hyperbaric oxygen therapy in ischaemic diabetic lower extremity ulcers: a double-blind randomised-controlled trial', *European journal of vascular and endovascular surgery*, Vol. 25, No. 6, (2003), pp. 513-518

[11] 38 out of 39 who completed the 30 sessions of hyperbaric oxygenation or were healed earlier had no amputation of any kind. 'At the end of the follow-up period, 31 patients (52%) in the SC group remained free of any amputation (i.e., including minor amputations), compared with 38 (63%) patients in the SC+HBOT group (RD 12% [95% CI −6 to 28]).' Santema, K.T., Stoekenbroek, R.M., Koelemay, M.J., Reekers, J.A., Van Dortmont, L.M., Oomen, A., Smeets, L., Wever, J.J., Legemate, D.A. and Ubbink, D.T., 'Hyperbaric oxygen therapy in the treatment of ischemic lower-extremity ulcers in patients with diabetes: results of the DAMO2CLES multicenter randomized clinical trial', *Diabetes Care*, Vol. 41, No. 1, (2018), pp. 112-19

evidence matrix is based on science. It's used for hypoxic tissue injury found in diseases, inflammation, infection and sepsis.[12] [13]

One will see later in the book that, in most countries, a victim's lawyer will only succeed in a legal case against a medical professional and/or hospital in disclosure and informed consent law if one can show cumulatively:

(a) that there was a failure to take reasonable care to make balanced disclosure (to explain) any material risk and/or reasonable alternative or variant treatment options and

(b) that the reasonable variant treatment option (of, for example, hyperbaric oxygenation, nutrition and/or fasting) or material risk was material in their care and

(c) that, if explained, the patient would not have taken the risk and/or would have used or taken the reasonable alternative treatment option. Importantly, what's reasonable is determined by the fact finder, such as a judge or jury, who can step into the shoes of the reasonable person in the patient's position as opposed to a medical expert's 'medical' view.

(d) that, based on the best evidence available at the time as determined by law, the treatment would have delivered a materially better outcome to the patient than otherwise, such that the patient suffered a harm.

---

[12] Memar, M.Y., Yekani, M., Alizadeh, N. and Baghi, H.B., 'Hyperbaric oxygen therapy: Antimicrobial mechanisms and clinical application for infections', *Biomedicine & Pharmacotherapy*, Vol. 109, (2019), pp. 440-47.

[13] Bærnthsen, N.F., Hansen, M.B., Wahl, A.M. et al. 'Treatment with 24 h–delayed normo- and hyperbaric oxygenation in severe sepsis induced by cecal ligation and puncture in rats', *Journal of Inflammation*, Vol. 14, No. 27, (2017). Available online at: https://doi.org/10.1186/s12950-017-0173-4

What is problematic for lawyers defending the medical community in a scenario where a medical professional is sued for failing to take reasonable care to make disclosure, is the actual scientific evidence or artillery in the victim's lawyer's hands. The known benefits for hyperbaric oxygenation are based on the universal gas laws. The problem with COVID-19 was that inflamed, injured and dysfunctional tissue was not receiving the oxygen required, so the dosage needed to be increased. Lawyers' tactics are described later in the book; however, one must see that for COVID-19 the tactics will be simple. A victim's lawyers will be able to cross-examine any defence expert witness using the evidence that, in medical or nursing schools, it is part of the curriculum to demonstrate that the method that delivers the highest dosage of oxygen to the whole body is increased pressure. There lies the problem in defending any case, as the known healing benefits are based on the universal gas laws. These laws may even sound familiar from science class in school. They are Boyle's law, Henry's law, Graham's law and Dalton's law.[14]

In a legal scenario, the victim's lawyer can show that their effect is undeniable. This presents a legal problem in defending the medical community. Unfortunately, a victim's lawyer could use a 12-year-old student's schoolbook on science to cross-examine a defence expert witness with impeachment or unseating evidence.

In the US, using previous damaging or incriminating evidence or information in a medical textbook or in medical reports is what

---

[14] The pressure (p) of a given quantity of gas varies inversely with its volume (v) at constant temperature (Boyle's law); Increasing the concentration of the oxygen inspired increases the plasma oxygen tension (Henry's law); Increasing the ambient pressure for a given percentage of oxygen inspired increases the partial pressure of the gas (Dalton's law); Increasing the plasma oxygen tension increases the gradient for oxygen transport to tissue (Graham's law).

lawyers for victims call 'impeachment' or 'unseating evidence'. It's used by victim's lawyers wishing to unseat or impeach a defence expert witness in cross-examination.

This route or tactic is similar in most jurisdictions. Nonetheless, this evidence is used to discredit the witness's evidence and persuade the fact finder, such as a judge or jury, that the witness's evidence is inconsistent with an earlier statement or treatments offered by the relevant hospital or other hospitals, or is inconsistent with published medical evidence, or with a book. It can be evidence to contradict one's previous statements or show that a witness is unqualified or being untruthful.

The same information about the universal gas laws is in every pre-med textbook and in every edition of the *Textbook of Hyperbaric Medicine* (K K Jain). For example, the pressure of a given quantity of gas varies inversely with its volume (Boyle's law). Increasing the plasma oxygen tension increases the gradient for oxygen transport to tissue (Graham's law). These are the reasons why the oxygen under pressure takes up less space and reaches into the plasma or injured tissue it may not have otherwise reached. When one comes right down to it, this is how the major oxygen debt problem with COVID-19 was rapidly resolved with hyperbaric oxygenation.[15]

Nonetheless, the similarity with COVID-19 symptoms and wound healing is that each condition has arterial insufficiency, hypoxic tissue injury at cellular level, hypoxemia (oxygen shortage) in the blood, inflammation and often sepsis (the blood's extreme response to infection). All of this shortage of oxygen with COVID-19 was causing tissue injury which was, in

[15] Ibid., Feldmeier, J.J., et al., 'Physiologic and biochemical rationale for treating COVID-19 patients with hyperbaric oxygen', (2021)

turn, causing cells to malfunction or even die in many parts of the body, including the lungs, the brain, the heart, the gastrointestinal tract, erectile function, the kidney and other organ tissue.[16] This was already known to the medical professionals in the Opelousas Hospital. I read about their success in news features and on television repeated on the Internet. I was at a loss and could not understand why the entire medical profession did not follow their lead.

I made contact with these healthcare professionals at Opelousas because I admired their leadership and thought they might help me persuade the leaders in the Irish authorities to follow their example.

In May 2020, their story of describing dramatic improvement was told to me on a WebEx video meeting with Nurse Marcus Speyrer and Dr Kerry Thibodeaux. A video conference call was arranged to be recorded to be sent to the Irish Minister for Health and the then Taoiseach (Prime Minister) who was, himself, a medical doctor and also to be sent to the COVID-19 Response Parliamentary Committee. They told the story of the recovery of the first patient. Because oxygenation at atmospheric pressure was insufficient, the patient's tachypnoea (rapid breathing) was deteriorating and the oxygen saturation readings were decreasing.

Something new had to be tried to help improve the odds of saving the life of a colleague and others in intensive care. The next treatment option was either invasive mechanical ventilation or hyperbaric oxygenation. Clinical reports from Wuhan, China, reported that it was safe and it worked. Obviously, the patients

---

[16] Chu, K.Y., Nackeeran, S., Horodyski, L., Masterson, T.A. and Ramasamy, R., 'COVID-19 infection is associated with new onset Erectile Dysfunction: Insights from a National Registry', *Sexual Medicine*, Vol. 10, No. 1, (2022), p. 10,0478

opted for hyperbaric oxygenation for 90 minutes each day in the chamber as a concurrent treatment when offered and the rest is history. Once in the hyperbaric chamber, the improvement in the rapid breathing or panting was clearly visible as well as improvements in the overall condition. The measurable blood saturation counts improved. The first patient is an example of (n=1), meaning one patient in a trial. There was a change for the better and this was expected. The nurse and four other patients treated with hyperbaric oxygenation were given either one session or up to six sessions as required.

**Question for Judge or Jury**

The legal and ethical question about the story so far in this chapter is: Would a judge or jury make a finding that a reasonable person in the patient's position would consider significant? Should the information have been disclosed to patients prior to giving a valid informed consent to any other medical treatment?

This discussion is equally about the medical community and hospital management who knew about the successful outcomes for COVID-19 patients who were treated with hyperbaric oxygenation. What's problematic for defence lawyers defending a hospital's position is that the legal right to be informed and make the decision to use this treatment option is, from a layperson's perspective, in the patient's position.

The volunteer Opelousas patients in Louisiana, US, were part of a trial that was published in a series case report called 'Hyperbaric oxygen therapy in preventing mechanical ventilation in COVID-19 patients: a retrospective case series', where (n=5) means five patients.17 Subsequently, all patients with COVID-19 in the Opelousas Hospital were offered hyperbaric oxygenation. The results in this US hospital replicated the results of the first two trials in published case reports from Wuhan, China, which were with one patient (n=1) (Zhong et al., 27 February 2020), and then five patients from hospitals in China (Chen et al., 8 April 2020), discussed later.[18] [19]

## Peer Reviews

While the layperson in the patient's position like those in Opelousas, Louisiana, is likely to have already opted for hyperbaric oxygenation, doctors are trained to seek out peer-reviewed case reports. In a legal scenario, disclosure of the *best* information at the time is the deciding factor. In court it would not be effective for a defence lawyer to say the doctors did not inform the patient because there were no peer reviews of a reported case at the time.

Nevertheless, a culture deep-rooted in the medical community, attributes importance to peer reviews of studies in the normal course of practice. In the course of this pandemic, however, anecdotal reports came before the published reports and were acted upon by some doctors, patients and hospital administrators and not by others.

---

[17] Thibodeaux K., Speyrer M., Raza A., Yaakov R., Serena T.E., 'Hyperbaric oxygen therapy in preventing mechanical ventilation in COVID-19 patients: a retrospective case series', *Journal of Wound Care*, Vol. 29, S4-S8, (2020). Available online at: https://pubmed.ncbi.nlm.nih.gov/32412891/

[18] Chen, R., Zhong, X., Tang, Y., Liang, Y., Li, B., Tao, X. and Liao, C., 'The outcomes of hyperbaric oxygen therapy to severe and critically ill patients with COVID-19 pneumonia', *Journal of SMMU Bajo Revisión*, (2020)

[19] Zhong, X., Tao, X., Tang, Y. and Chen, R., 'The outcomes of hyperbaric oxygen therapy to retrieve hypoxemia of severe novel coronavirus pneumonia: first case report', *Zhonghua Hanghai Yixue yu Gaoqiya Yixue Zazhi*, (2020)

The difficulty for defence lawyers defending the interest of the medical community is that, at all times and understandably so in a pandemic, the best evidence available at the time must be explained to patients. With the emphasis on 'at the time', one cannot allow people to die while waiting for randomised controlled trials. If some doctors had concerns about perceived risks involved for both the patient and the health workers, this is not a defence from withholding information. The legal issue is that if the doctor did not want to take the risk, then the patient should have been told about the treatment nonetheless.

In any event, the initial reviews of the first clinical report (Zhong, et al.) from China was independently reviewed by a series of experts. The first two were Professor Philip James, Department of Surgery, University of Dundee, Scotland, UK, and Professor Paul Harch, Department of Medicine, Section of Emergency and Hyperbaric Medicine, Louisiana State University Health Sciences Center, New Orleans, Louisiana, US.[20] In Professor James's letter to the editor, he pointed to earlier reports supporting the scientific basis that the findings in China were sound and stated: 'Tissue hypoxia leads to further inflammation from the attraction of neutrophils. The vicious cycle where inflammation is tied to hypoxia can only be broken by an increase in the oxygen available to tissue.'

In the US, De Maio et al. published a peer review report in May 2020, which included the reports from China already

---

[20] Paul G Harch,

1. 'Hyperbaric oxygen treatment of novel coronavirus (COVID-19) respiratory failure', pp. 61-62 (available online at: https://www.medgasres.com/text.asp?2020/10/2/61/282177 [cited February 9, 2022]), and

2. 'Intermittent high dosage oxygen treats COVID-19 infection: the Chinese studies', p. 5 in *Medical Gas Research*, Vol. 10, No. 2 (2020).

mentioned and outlined why hyperbaric oxygenation is a treatment: ‘A small study from China has shown excellent potential for its use in the treatment of COVID-19 patients in this study, five critically ill patients with COVID-19 and signs of hypoxia were subjected to HBOT. After two treatments, a dramatic improvement in the clinical condition of the patients was observed with an increase in blood oxygen saturation level and reduced lung inflammation, as observed by CT scans.’[21] [22] This report from De Maio gave a link for the earlier reports from China (Chen et al.).

**Media and Food and Drug Administration**

The media in Louisiana and elsewhere in the US reported the success of Dr Thibodeau and his team. In August 2020, a story on hyperbaric oxygenation and the COVID-19 pandemic was featured on multi-platform networks on television across all 52 states in the US and the Internet. One introduction to the broadcast said the journalist investigated ‘whether it really works and why it hasn’t been used more often’. TV anchor and investigative reporter, Mr Duane Pohlman, narrated that: ‘More than a dozen hospitals across the country say hyperbaric oxygen therapy (HBOT) is saving the lives of even the most critically ill coronavirus patients.’[23] Experts were interviewed and they explained the known benefits and why it was working on COVID-19.

---

[21] ‘Demonstration report on inclusion of hyperbaric oxygen therapy in treatment of COVID-19 severe cases’, Naval Specialty Medical Center Program Team, (June 2020). Available online at: https://www.ncbi.nlm.nih.gov/pmc/articles/PMC7885707/

[22] De Maio, A. and Hightower, L.E., ‘COVID-19, acute respiratory distress syndrome (ARDS), and hyperbaric oxygen therapy (HBOT): what is the link?’, *Cell Stress and Chaperones*, Vol. 25, (2020), pp.717-20.

[23] Ibid., Pohlman, ‘New treatment promises hope during pandemic’, *Local 12*, (2020). ‘From Louisiana to Long Island, hyperbaric chambers, once used only to treat divers

Information given on the TV programme may become legally problematic for the Food and Drug Administration. Mr Pohlman placed an article on-screen called 'Don't Be Misled' and put the administration under the spotlight. The Food and Drug Administration used the expression 'not established' and, unfortunately, listed medical conditions (including neurological conditions such as brain damage) that hyperbaric oxygenation is the standard of care for in many parts of the world and often paid for by public and private health insurance. The legal problem for the Food and Drug Administration is that this could be considered to be the tort of negligent misrepresentation. Was this government agency using the expression 'Don't Be Misled' to dissuade people or other providers from using this treatment option?

The greatly respected researchers of Aviv Clinics in Florida and Dubai, who published research in *Traumatic Brain Injury*, were inspired because of the powerfully provable benefits for the injured tissue in the brain. Unfortunately, it would be impeachment or unseating evidence against the interests of a medical professional if the Food and Drug Administration's incorrect information was given in a face-to-face medical consultation, because it's not balanced or accurate.

The journalists making the TV programme did their job well. The television attention seemed to have influenced the Food and Drug Administration in 2020; it removed the article from its website, as did other hospitals (but not all), that contained the same misleading information. The article stated: 'Patients may be unaware that the safety and effectiveness of HBOT has not been established for these

---

suffering from the bends, are increasingly being used to treat COVID-19 patients with surprising success.' https://www.youtube.com/watch?v=Vwd9rLVhmYI

diseases and conditions...'[24] Notwithstanding the fact that the Food and Drug Administration made this statement, the officials may not be aware that in Europe, under the European Convention for the Protection of Human Rights and Dignity of the Human Being, people are entitled under Article 5 to balanced information before *any* medical intervention.[25]

## The Conundrum of an Underused Treatment

Despite media coverage and the published clinical case series reports, by February 2022, the conundrum was: despite the success, why have a reported total of 16,044 people died of COVID-19 in Louisiana? The challenge is to understand why hyperbaric oxygenation patients were not informed and this treatment option was underused.

Unfortunately, well-intentioned doctors wrongly advocated (even before the pandemic) that there must be proof by randomised controlled trials with a control group before recommending a treatment option to a patient. I will explain later why it was wrongly advocated in the Cochrane Reviews due to the provisions of the Nuremberg Code, which explains when humans can't be randomised for an experiment.

I will quote here from an email, to help one understand why there was a refusal to inform patients about hyperbaric oxygenation as a treatment option. One may ask why the medical

---

[24] This was the link to the offending article: https://www.fda.gov/consumers/consumer-updates/hyperbaric-oxygen-therapy-dont-be-misled

[25] Convention for the Protection of Human Rights and Dignity of the Human Being, with regard to 'Application of Biology and Medicine: Convention on Human Rights and Biomedicine', Article 5 – 'General rule: An intervention in the health field may only be carried out after the person concerned has given free and informed consent to it. This person shall beforehand be given appropriate information as to the purpose and nature of the intervention as well as on its consequences and risks. The person concerned may freely withdraw consent at any time.'

community did not just copy hospitals in the US and China and start offering hyperbaric oxygenation. One has an example to explain the delay or what was a barrier to using hyperbaric oxygenation. This illustration was contained in an email from a medical leader in anaesthesiology working for the Irish Health Service Executive. Regrettably, this decent hardworking doctor proved himself in the email to be unwittingly unaware of the law governing what must be disclosed to patients (what is their right to know) and, further, what level of clinical evidence is required for the delivery of treatment options in a pandemic. This person's actions unfortunately epitomised those in hospital management who were also unaware of medical laws.

On reading this email, the question one should ask is: Will the scenario of requiring a randomised controlled trial before using the National Hyperbaric Medicine Unit at University Hospital Galway withstand logical analysis by a court? The legal question is: Will a non-medical person after giving the email due consideration see how the reasoning was flawed logically, medically and legally?

Will the scenario in the email separately withstand logical analysis by considering the inconsistencies or contradictions by specifying a need for a randomised controlled trial on the one hand for hyperbaric oxygenation, and then not specifying a need for a randomised controlled trial on the other for using mechanical ventilators for oxygenation?

This person's email, unfortunately, also showed noncompliance with the Irish Department of Health's published guidelines for medical interventions, *Ethical Framework for Decision-making in a Pandemic*, as regards using the best evidence available at the time.

Obviously, from the content of the email, it was clear that patients were not being told about the known benefits of hyperbaric oxygenation. Another obvious inconsistency was apparent from Twitter that drugs were used globally for critically ill patients from COVID-19 without any randomised controlled trials.

Unfortunately, from a legal and a humanitarian perspective, the doctor wrote in his email on 12 June 2020: 'Dear Mr Lynch, I'm happy to reconsider my opinion if you have any randomised controlled clinical trial data showing hyperbaric oxygen to improve the survival of critically patients with COVID-19 induced respiratory failure. Please do send on any published papers that you have to this effect.' If one agrees with this position taken about a randomised controlled trial, then in this case one is legally wrong.

As a result of this email from a Health Service Executive employee, will the Irish Health Service Executive be found in a legal scenario to have caused adverse medical events due to ignorance of the law? Was this scenario due to taking a legally wrong position regarding not deploying the Hyperbaric Medicine Unit in University Hospital Galway for avoiding the increased risks of all COVID-19 and Long COVID-19 complications, including deaths?

After the first case (n=1) in Wuhan, China (replicated in Louisiana), and the lessons from historical law cases on disclosure, a victim's lawyer has ample evidence to show material that there was no ethical or legal justification for randomising humans for experimentation, beginning with the reasons in the Nuremberg Code. A victim's lawyer will point to the scientific, ethical and legal reasons as to why it's a mistake and inconsequential in a legal scenario to refer to the (n=1) cases as evidence identified as low quality.

**Ethical Framework in Ireland**

A further legal problem for those wanting higher quality evidence is that, in Ireland, the Department of Health reported the ethics correctly. They published ethical guidelines in March 2020 called *Ethical Framework for Decision-making in a Pandemic.* The ethical guidelines on page 9 state, 'decisions should be based on the best available evidence at the time', and on page 15 state: 'consideration of how benefit can be maximised will include reference to the best clinical evidence available at the time.'

Unfortunately for those calling for randomised controlled trials for COVID-19, they are mistaken due to the articles of the post-World War II Nuremberg Code. I quote the pivotal reference from the British Medical Journal, which at paragraph 2 states: 'The experiment should be such as to yield fruitful results for the good of society, unprocurable by other methods or means of study, and not random and unnecessary in nature.'

I quoted paragraph 2 of the Code because all too many people in the medical community said that (n=1) was sufficient and there was no need for clinical trials before informing people about this option.

No person would want to be in the controlled group and risk death and the chronic symptoms of Long COVID. In addition, no person should be asked to be in the controlled group. The Nuremberg Code is clear about disclosure and informed consent when it states:

> *The voluntary consent of the human subject is absolutely essential. This means that the person involved should have the legal capacity to give consent; should be so situated as to be able to exercise free power of choice, without the intervention of any element of force, fraud, deceit, duress, overreaching, or other ulterior forms of constraint or coercion; and should have sufficient knowledge and comprehension of the elements of the subject matter involved as to enable him to make an understanding and enlightened decision.*

The next medico-legal problem relates to the drugs approval agencies, such as the Food and Drug Administration in the United States seeking randomised controlled trials. It's the same for those seeking and giving ethical approval. One must seriously consider the possible loss of one single life that could occur in the controlled group in a COVID-19 human experiment. Even if the results using hyperbaric oxygenation in China and or Louisiana were not known, the benefits of using hyperbaric oxygenation for replacing the oxygen debt found in COVID-19 were known.

To support the case of (n=1) corroborative or collateral scientific evidence supporting why and how it works has been explained. Nonetheless, this scientific evidence is a medical view, whereas what matters in a legal scenario is what the layperson in the patient's position would consider significant information. Put another way, if one was seriously or critically ill with COVID-19, is the disclosure (information) in the earlier part of this chapter from Louisiana and China enough for one to want non-invasive hyperbaric oxygenation as opposed to invasive mechanical ventilation?

The medical community and public may ask, once the above information does become known, 'is it true that people died unnecessarily in the COVID-19 pandemic?' A further question is: 'Was a reasonable and successful treatment option properly disclosed to both the legal and ethical standards required?'

**Doctors Conflicted**

On a red flag subject of being 'conflicted', some doctors are conflicted or may be biased in a legal sense in several ways. I don't want to divert attention from the main message in this book, which is the value of balanced disclosure and a valid informed consent to the entire medical community and their patients.

However, I have been made aware by several concerned members of the medical or scientific community, of controversies between doctors and/or between university departments. Because drug companies were funding university hospitals all over the world to conduct trials for research purposes to seek evidence for a cure for their drug for symptoms of COVID-19, patients were needed for these human experiments.

I was told of a hospital in Canada where patients were said to be 'pre-booked' for a drug company trial. I was told that this arrangement of 'pre-booking' patients was normal in university hospitals. In another anecdote, I was informed that doctors in the intensive care departments of two hospitals would not send their COVID-19 patients for hyperbaric oxygenation treatments as part of clinical trials despite the known benefits. What is of concern in all this is that the patients may not have been given balanced information on treatment options.

Continuing the subject on being conflicted in a legal scenario, there is also another subpopulation of doctors who may be exposed on cross-examination. Any doctor who treated seriously ill COVID-19 patients and did not give balanced disclosure information on treatment options is conflicted in this discussion. Authors of review articles may also be conflicted if they took part in randomised experimental trials on humans for COVID-19 despite the known benefits.

I flag here again the Nuremberg Code and the European Convention on Human Rights on the ethics and illegality of unnecessary randomised controlled trials on humans. This unfortunate story of 'pre-booked' patients, while normal in university hospitals, is in danger of being determined by a court as unlawful and offending against the Nuremberg Code. The concerns explained to me are retold here to help the medical community realise that what is normal clinical practice is likely to be determined as unlawful.

If one thinks that the practice of arranging 'pre-booked' patients without disclosure about hyperbaric oxygenation (as appears to have happened here) is not a failure to give balanced disclosure and is not a failure to obtain a valid informed consent, then in this case, one is wrong.

**Translation from Chinese**

The story behind the first reported clinical trial by Thibodeaux in Louisiana in the US was influenced by Dr Paul Harch, the American physician. He is an author, also based in Louisiana and a colleague of Dr Thibodeaux. By publishing information on the first successes in China, Dr Harch gave the first light at the end of the tunnel. He gave hope for a treatment for the seriously ill COVID-19 patients by showing how injured tissue caused by COVID-19 has recovered using hyperbaric oxygenation. Dr Harch is in clinical practice. He is a Clinical Professor, Department of Internal Medicine Director, Medical Center of Louisiana Hyperbaric

Medicine Department. Dr Harch was the first President of the International Hyperbaric Medicine Association.

In my research for this book, I learned that there is contention and a different outlook on using hyperbaric oxygenation between this association and another international group of experts in the Undersea Hyperbaric Medical Society (UHMS).

In any event, on 11 March 2020, Dr Harch, having analysed the research after exchanges with the clinicians in China, advocated the use of hyperbaric oxygenation for COVID-19 patients.

The Undersea Hyperbaric Medical Society published a medical review in 2021 called 'Physiologic and biochemical rationale for treating COVID-19 patients with hyperbaric oxygen'.26

However, when Dr Harch first wrote on social media about the lifesaving information in the study from China, on that same day there was a recorded 39 deaths in total from COVID-19 in the US. With what seems to me to be great foresight, Dr Harch and his team helped his Chinese colleagues translate their studies into English. Dr Harch also wrote to political leaders in the US, but they were being, as I see it, unfortunately and inappropriately advised in this instance to ask for randomised controlled trials. While this response from the politicians may seem like 'good science', I would venture the opinion that it was not so.

Obviously, delay for randomised trials would mean more people would die in the pandemic. Nevertheless, legally problematic for those who advised the politicians, people were dying by the thousands per day and more were critically ill, and

[26] Ibid., Feldmeier, J.J. et al. 'Physiologic and biochemical rationale for treating COVID-19 patients with hyperbaric oxygen', (2021), pp. 1-12

the best evidence available *at the time* may not have been fully outlined and explained to the politicians.

In addition to writing a peer review letter, Professor James also wrote to the British Prime Minister, the American President and to the Irish Parliamentary COVID-19 Response Committee about why he felt hyperbaric oxygenation should be used immediately for treatment of COVID-19.

## More about Clinical Trials being Unlawful and Unethical

What is also legally problematic for those who called for randomised controlled trials is that Professor Ruiyong Chen in China, who co-authored the first two published studies with Professor Philip James in the UK, separately wrote that clinical trials were both unnecessary and would be unethical. This was based on the view that patients would be deprived of the known benefits. Professor Chen wrote in a letter to me in April 2020 that I passed to the Undersea Hyperbaric Medical Society in the US: 'I think the clinical trial is to violate Hippocratic Oath to set patients with obvious hypoxia as control without a definitely useful treatment.' My understanding of Professor Chen's words is that a clinical trial would be unethical and there was no other useful or better treatment than hyperbaric oxygenation. The control group with obvious hypoxia (shortage of oxygen at the cellular level that can cause death) should not be deprived of the known benefits of hyperbaric oxygenation.

Adding to this debate, but not on the subject of COVID-19, (Dr) Joseph Maroon MD FACS, who did the 60 hyperbaric oxygenation cycle of sessions and assessments at Aviv Clinics in Florida, quoted a Harvard professor in an article:

*In 1976, William Sweet, professor of neurosurgery and chairman at Harvard, wrote, 'I believe we have become excessively imbued with the conviction that multiple consonant observations are necessary before even tentative conclusions can be drawn from biological phenomena, that a randomized statistically significant series is necessary for firm conclusions ... We need to establish faith and the capacity of the biologist to reach a valid novel conception on the basis of one single set of facts. There is a staggering difference between zero and one when the one is a good idea.'*[27]

This point of view raises several questions: Is this Harvard professor suggesting that typical medical procedures could lead to delay in implementing a perfectly good treatment and result in the unnecessary deaths of patients? Is this Harvard professor begging the doctors to change the way they practice and to tell their patients about the scientific reasons for the benefits, even if (n=1)? However, since 1972 in the US, the law of disclosure and informed consent was that one must under legal obligation take reasonable care to disclose the treatment options based on the best evidence available at the time.

## The First Patient in China

The story about the first patient treated in China (n=1) was recounted to me by Professor Ruiyong Chen, a senior officer in the Chinese Navy in the Diving and Hyperbaric Medicine

[27] Joseph Maroon, 'My Personal Journey to Florida's Aviv Hyperbaric Clinic', Joseph C. Maroon, MD, FACS, (January 2022). Available online at: https://www.josephmaroon.com/blog/hyperbaric-oxygen-better-brain-health/

Department of Naval Medical Center, Naval Medical University, Shanghai, China.[28]

Dr Chen helped me understand the controversy and sent me correspondence for publication as part of humankind's fight against the virus. The background to the story is that the patient referred to as 'Tang xx' in the first report was a critically ill 69-year-old man. As it happened, he was admitted the day before the first day of the Wuhan lockdown.

In Dr Chen's email, he stated that: 'When this new coronavirus was not understood, in China in January, many news reports made me feel that hypoxemia is an important issue according to my knowledge in the hyperbaric physiology. I recommended to her [Dr Zhong] to try hyperbaric oxygen.' Dr Chen continued, 'but it wasn't used until 11th February, at which time her husband was critically ill when she made her decision to use hyperbaric oxygenation'. This was the 23rd day after being admitted to the hospital. There were already 1,113 COVID-19 deaths in China on the first day that 'Tang xx' had hyperbaric oxygenation.

The results were reported by the doctors to be amazing. After the first session, it's reported that the 'dyspnoea' (difficult or laboured breathing or panting), chest pain and gastrointestinal symptoms improved significantly.

From a legal scenario perspective, biological or scientific evidence taken before, during and after treatments can be combined with similar timings of lung CT scans. Because lack of

---

[28] Col Chen is a Professor from China. He graduated from Second Military Medical University Of PLA, China. Since 1997 he has been employed in the Naval Medical Research Institute of PLA. He was in the Diving and Submarine Escape Medical Research and Support for China Navy and got his medical degree in July 2005. Information can be sourced online here: http://www.cimm-icmm.org/page/anglais/Malaysian_abstract/Concurrent%20Session%202.pdf

oxygenation in the blood was one of the measures of being critically ill, as standard care doctors monitor the percentages of dissolved oxygen in the blood. From a legal proof view, the clinical evidence of recovery supported the already known benefits of using hyperbaric oxygenation.

When Zhong et al. published, it gave much hope and a powerful sense of relief in humanity's war against this virus attacking the world. The subsequent peer-reviewed reports from around the world verified the first (n=1) report from China. In any event, this peer-reviewed report was published in the *Chinese Journal of Nautical Medicine and Hyperbaric Medicine*. The report was completed before the eighth and last hyperbaric session on this first patient.[29]

In this discussion, it's important to understand that before Dr Zhong's single case report was published, the administrative authorities in China took quick action based on anecdotal clinical information. The authorities decided to add a hyperbaric chamber unit to the new military Huoshenshan Hospital in Wuhan.[30] This was the military hospital reported about and seen on televisions around the world that had just been built in a 10-day window between 23 January 2020 and 2 February 2020. In further record time, the construction of the new hyperbaric oxygenation medical unit took 15 days to be installed and put into use.

However, severely or critically ill people were treated with hyperbaric oxygenation in three of Wuhan's hospitals, and 100% of those treated that Dr Chen knew of survived. Nonetheless,

---

[29] Zhong X., Tao X., Tang Y., et al., 'Hyperbaric oxygen therapy to correct hypoxia in patients with severe new coronavirus pneumonia: the first report', *Chinese Journal of Nautical Medicine and Hyperbaric Medicine*, Vol. 27, (2020). Available online at: http://rs.yiigle.com/yufabiao/1182641.htm. DOI: 10.3760 / cma.j.issn.1009-6906.2020.0001

[30] 'How can China build a hospital in 10 days?', New China TV, (2020). Available online at: https://www.youtube.com/watch?v=OWp6vSHFG4M

because seriously and critically ill patients were successfully treated with hyperbaric oxygenation, it's important to ask why 13,195 people were reported by the Johns Hopkins Coronavirus Resource Centre to have died in China of COVID-19 by the date 8 April 2022.31 Even in China, the same conundrum arose because, obviously, some doctors in the same hospitals with hyperbaric chambers must not have informed their severely or critically ill COVID-19 patients about the known benefits of the hyperbaric oxygenation option.

The military hospital with the new hyperbaric oxygenation department was closed on 15 April 2020, after only 12 weeks of use, because not enough patients were seriously ill with COVID-19 and there was the perception that there was no more need for its availability and use.

All of this information was the best clinical evidence available at the time, reporting on the best outcomes in the world for survival of critically ill COVID-19 patients.

At an important time in May 2020, the Minister and Secretary General of the Department of Health in Ireland were included in exchanges of emails between world experts from the US, the UK, Ireland, Poland and with Professor Chen. These emails included discussions on the known benefits of hyperbaric oxygenation for COVID-19. It was hoped that in addition to the Hyperbaric Medicine Unit at Galway University Hospital being used for COVID-19, other private pressure cabins in Ireland, such as those on Irish Navy ships and at the Haulbowline Irish naval base in County Cork, could have been deployed on an emergency basis. This did not happen and hyperbaric oxygenation was not used by

---

31 This figure was obtained from the Johns Hopkins Coronavirus Recourse Centre and is available online at: https://coronavirus.jhu.edu/region/china

the Irish authorities for COVID-19 up to the time of completing this book in August 2022.

It remains for a judge or an inquest to determine if balanced information on this subject was disclosed to patients before obtaining informed consent.

### Undersea Hyperbaric Medical Society's Influence on the Irish Department of Health

On 22 May 2020, I received an email from an official in the Irish Department of Health's COVID-19 Response Team. I apologise for publishing this email to the people who have suffered the tragedies of this pandemic that took the lives of loved ones. I apologise if one is shocked and angry by the dismissal by the Department of Health of a treatment that was, at the time, the best-known treatment option with the best results. The email was copied to the Irish Minister for Health, the Secretary-General of the Department, and a number of other officials and others. The correspondence is available under the Freedom of Information Act.

The legal problem for lawyers defending the emergency medicine doctors is that the treating doctors making decisions may have overlooked the law which is that: It's a judge who will decide by putting him or herself in the patient's position to determine what should have been disclosed. The judge will also decide whether or not the Nuremberg Code or the ethical guidelines of the Department of Health for a pandemic are followed by applying 'the best available evidence at the time'.

The email on 22 May 2020 from the COVID-19 Response Team on the next page states:

*'Dear Mr Lynch,*

*I refer to your correspondence received by the Department of Health, including the Secretary General's Office referring to the use of Hyperbaric Oxygen for COVID-19 patients. Thank you for your offer of assistance. We are grateful of the extent of goodwill from businesses and organisations who are eager to help since the coronavirus (COVID-19) outbreak in Ireland.*

*The HSE Medicines Management Programme has examined the evidence for the role of hyperbaric oxygen therapy in the management and treatment of COVID-19. The department has been advised that there is a lack of robust published clinical evidence to support the use of hyperbaric oxygen therapy (HBOT) for the treatment of COVID-19. The limited evidence identified was of low quality, comprising case reports of small patient numbers. In addition, the HSE HBOT programme has confirmed that while there are some case reports and some clinical trials underway internationally, there appear to be conflicting reports and insufficient high-quality data to recommend HBOT as a standard of care in COVID-19 patients. Information was also reviewed from the Undersea Hyperbaric Medical Society (UHMS), which also indicated that there is insufficient evidence to endorse the use of routine adjunctive HBO2 for COVID-19 patients outside the context of an IRB-approved clinical trial.*

*Thank you again for your contact, and I trust that this clarifies the position for you.*

*Kind Regards.'*

The email is signed off by a named public servant on the COVID-19 Response Team in the Department of Health. Unfortunately for the medical community in a legal scenario, this letter only adds to the problems of the defence lawyers. A victim's lawyer will successfully use the Department's ethical framework and argue that it was not applied. The known clinical evidence should have been disclosed. Whether or not it was peer-reviewed was not relevant to the law of disclosure and informed consent. It's not an excuse to wait around for some form of official treatment.

If a medical professional in consultation with a critically ill patient from COVID-19 thinks that one is safe from the artillery of a victim's lawyer by repeating this information in the Department's letter above, then in this case, the doctor would be wrong, as more information was required. The point is that a victim's lawyer will argue that if a medical professional prior to any medical intervention such as mechanical ventilation oxygenation failed to disclose to a critically ill patient information about the already known benefits of hyperbaric oxygenation as a treatment option, then there lies the problem. It can invalidate informed consent. One has to predict whether or not a judge or jury would determine that there was an invalid informed consent.

It's valuable to again consider the Nuremberg Code and waiting for an IRB-approved clinical trial to happen when all lives were saved in the clinical reports already published. Victim's lawyers will exploit to their advantage the language used in the email letter, such as the statement that there is 'a lack of robust published clinical evidence' and 'insufficient high-quality data to recommend hyperbaric oxygenation'. If one thinks that this is legally the appropriate reason for a decision to not tell a patient in a pandemic the best evidence available at the time, in this case, one is wrong based on the law of disclosure and informed consent. This is discussed further, later in this book. If the officials think they are legally following the Irish Department of Health's ethical guidelines on the best evidence available at the time for the pandemic, then in this case, they are wrong.[32]

**Review by Coroner or Jury at Inquest**

Investigating the circumstances of how a death occurred is the role of the coroner or jury at an inquest. By way of example in this true story, an inquest jury found a verdict of death by misadventure of Ms Savita Halappanavar and her unborn baby following a septic miscarriage in 2013 in Ireland. It's valuable to understand the COVID-19 treatment controversy in the context of that inquest, as low oxygen concentration, septic shock and death is relevant to both. What's essential for the medical community to understand is that a coroner or a jury at an inquest around the world may add recommendations or 'riders' as they are known. One should pause here. One should see the red flag issue for the medical community, because what one may not understand is that this is the legalised role of laypersons. The layperson's jury tells medical professionals in the context of patients dying how they might or might not do their work in the future.

The issue of disclosure of treatment options and invalid informed consent will be used by victims' lawyers so could be the subject of riders, therefore lessons can be learned. Very soon in the COVID-19 controversy, what's problematic is that this could

---

[32] 'Ethical framework for decision-making in a pandemic From Department of Health', published at: https://www.gov.ie/en/publication/dbf3fb-ethical-framework-for-decision-making-in-a-pandemic/ (27 March 2020, updated 17 April 2020).

be about the need for oversight of disclosure and valid informed consent management.

Hyperbaric oxygenation was available at the hospital where Ms Halappanavar died, however, it was not used on that occasion for the sepsis.

In a Health Information and Quality Authority report surrounding the death of Ms Halappanavar, it stated that 'clinical observations include measuring blood pressure, heart rate, temperature, rate of respiration, oxygen saturation'.[33] However, these were not monitored to the satisfaction of the Authority. As regards low oxygen saturation and sepsis, we know that hyperbaric oxygenation is a likely additional treatment option of choice for the patient if the information is disclosed prior to an informed consent. The report also said the University Hospital Galway reported that '167 maternity and non-maternity patients in total required ICU care as a result of sepsis in 2011 and 139 patients in 2012 ... Despite this, the Authority found that at the time of the investigation, the hospital did not have a hospital-wide guideline in place for the management of sepsis in adult patients.' The report also said that: 'The Saving Mothers Lives 2011 report identified that mortality due to severe maternal sepsis was the leading cause of direct maternal death in the UK.' What is problematic to this day is that the use of hyperbaric oxygenation for sepsis is not part of the clinical guidelines. It should be used for sepsis and MRSA because it would help the medical community comply with the law on disclosure and informed consent.

---

[33] Investigation into the safety, quality and standards of services provided by the Health Service Executive to patients, including pregnant women, at risk of clinical deterioration, including those provided in University Hospital Galway, and as reflected in the care and treatment provided to Savita Halappanavar.

In addition to low oxygen and sepsis, an issue to be considered is that in a book by Kewal K Jain in its sixth edition called *Textbook of Hyperbaric Medicine*, there is a full chapter on 'Hyperbaric Oxygenation in Obstetrics and Gynaecology'. Again, the reasonable person test applies to whether a judge would consider that a woman in danger of losing a baby would consider the known information about hyperbaric oxygenation significant. The textbook gives cases on the successful outcomes using hyperbaric oxygenation in other countries for threatened abortion, foetal hypoxia or to help the membrane protein composition. There are many case studies in past decades with examples of the application of hyperbaric oxygenation bringing the pregnancy to the full term. In this discussion, it's important for the medical community to be cautious and not rush to conclusions, and it's equally important not to express any view without considering all the evidence.

A Royal Canadian Navy medical doctor who, at the time, was retired and is an expert in hyperbaric medicine, came to my office at the time of the Ms Halappanavar inquest. I was given a hard copy of a case report from the Whipps Cross University Hospital in London, published in 1974. It reported the use of hyperbaric oxygenation for a pregnant woman with sepsis in similar circumstances.[34]

What would be problematic for a defence lawyer in terms of the law of disclosure is that this information was on the Internet and was not new, as the Whipps Cross University Hospital's report referenced an earlier study published in the Lancet in 1966

[34] Hanson, G.C., 'Septicaemic shock. Report of three cases: a review of diagnosis and management', Postgraduate Medical Journal, Vol. 50, No. 583, (1974), p. 288

on 26 cases of the treatment of clostridial infections with hyperbaric oxygenation.[35]

In March 2022, having considered the published evidence on the inquest and the inquiry, this doctor is still of the view that hyperbaric oxygenation should have been offered to Ms Halappanavar to help with her treatment. Importantly, his opinion is that, based on the Whipps Cross University Hospital report alone, hyperbaric oxygenation should be part of the hospital's clinical practice guidelines.

It's a red flag issue for the medical community to understand that this information is about how someone like Ms Halappanavar has a right to be told of the risk involved in not using hyperbaric oxygenation and therefore may want to try it. Nobody can say for certain what would have been the outcome. Therefore, before making a comment on this sepsis issue, what one says could be used as unseating evidence against the interests of a defendant. One should actually read the reported cases on the subject and think of the legal obligation to consider the reasonable person test.

The legal question for the coroner or a jury in the future could be: If this treatment option for sepsis and low oxygen levels was disclosed to Ms Halappanavar prior to an informed consent, would the chances of her survival have increased? The point is that it's not unreasonable to ask: Would the unborn baby and/or the mother be alive today?

The truth should be told to any inquest about the successes of the layperson volunteers from the local scuba diving club, who operated the hyperbaric chamber since its establishment in 1976

---

[35] Brummelkamp, W.H., Boerema, I. and Hoogendyk, L., 'Treatment of Clostridial Infections with Hyperbaric Oxygen Drenching a Report On 26 Cases', *The Lancet*, Vol. 281, No. 7275, (1963), pp. 235-238

at University Hospital Galway. The volunteers have used it successfully like the Opelousas Wound Treatment Center in Louisiana to prevent limb amputations. Over the years, the volunteers have also used it for potentially fatal conditions such as infections, sepsis, necrotising fasciitis, gas gangrene and lupus. However, this pivotal evidence of what could have been done for the infection leading to sepsis was not given at the Savita Halappanavar inquest. Neither was such evidence given to the Health Information and Quality Authority.

A rider for the inquest jury for COVID-19 may suggest that clinical practice guidelines should be based on science and informed consent and include the emergency administration of hyperbaric oxygenation in the event of low oxygen concentration, hypoxemia, hypoxia and suspected sepsis.

A further rider could be that if these guidelines were in place to use hyperbaric oxygenation, the treatments for COVID-19 would have been different and more lives saved. The doctors in University Hospital Galway have been trying to obtain funds to enhance the service.

### Long COVID-19 Syndrome and Treatments

Hope is justified for people with Long COVID-19 conditions. These next five pages may be the best news and allow one to judge if hyperbaric oxygenation is in reality the best current treatment option. Based on the scientific evidence, especially for those who are currently troubled about persistent neurological dysfunction (brain damage), hyperbaric oxygenation is likely to be one's treatment of choice.

Similar to COVID-19, Long COVID-19 condition has affected many of one's body functions, including (but not limited to) the neurological, respiratory, gastrointestinal, cardiovascular and musculoskeletal systems. It will be seen later in this book how all these systems, when attacked by hypoxic (shortage of oxygen) tissue injury at cellular level that resulted in disease, have (before the pandemic) been treated with hyperbaric oxygenation. The good news in the case reports, referenced later, is how there were significant improvements using hyperbaric oxygenation for people with memory loss, declined cognitive function, taste, smell, fatigue, depression or stroke-like symptoms such as balance, motor functions, slurring of words and headaches.

Again, medical professionals make disclosure about this treatment option for Long COVID-19 conditions, while others still do not. In a legal scenario, the same logical analysis applies. Based on a scientific matrix of evidence, one can show why those seriously ill with COVID-19 or Long COVID-19 conditions have significantly benefited from hyperbaric oxygenation.

The World Health Organisation (WHO) called it 'post-COVID-19 condition' if it persisted for more than 12 weeks. However, legally, it was problematic for one to be waiting 12 weeks before taking action to start using hyperbaric oxygenation, as it was exposing people to increased risks of avoidable post-COVID-19 complications. One can use logical analysis to show that too much time elapsing before using hyperbaric oxygenation is increasing the risk of complications. After all, living cells hold one's memory or control motor functions. A single cell can drown and die due to the cell leaking fluid, a symptom of hypoxia and inflammation. On the other hand, an almost drowned (dormant) cell, if given hyperbaric oxygenation, can be revived.

Similar biological phenomena in an evidence matrix can be shown, such as persistent tissue injury and persistent inflammation caused by the viral attack during infection. What's important legally and medically is to see that the biological phenomena can be delayed, and one can experience new Long COVID-19 symptoms after the infection period is over. In fact, many patients around the globe were still in intensive care units for weeks or even months after being oxygenated with mechanical ventilators, and yet their condition was deteriorating like a progressive disease even after they were no longer infected with the virus.

As stated earlier in medical terminology, the COVID-19 viral attack on cells promotes a downregulation (reduction at the cellular level) of proinflammatory cytokines and oxygenation under increased pressure reduces inflammation by healing injured cells.[36] Regrettably, many people who were considered to have been asymptomatic (showing no symptoms) were not in reality. They unhappily had delayed onset of symptoms caused by tissue injury in different organs. One is sorry to say that a victim's lawyer will be able to prove that their client was not informed about the known benefits of hyperbaric oxygenation and was exposed to increased risk of delayed and avoidable complications from Long COVID-19 syndrome.

Unfortunately, a victim's lawyer will be able to show that anyone giving the matter reasonable consideration will see that COVID-19 was known to be a viral attack causing hypoxic tissue injury at a cellular level. Scientists reported an out-of-control inflammation cycle (a cytokine storm). Of relevance to Long COVID-19 is that the medical coded language used in early reports describing the viral impact referred to hypoxaemia (shortage of oxygen in the blood) and hypoxia (shortage of oxygen in the tissue). There was a close to universal consensus that there was tissue injury, tissue damage, cell stress and/or lung tissue damage,

[36] Some cytokines stimulate the immune system and others slow it down.

and that these biological phenomena equally apply to Long COVID-19. Put another way, this inflammation created a storm or vicious cycle of more inflammation that continued like the progression of any traumatic injury or disease even when the infection had left the body. The person becomes free of the viral infection, but the damage is done and the hypoxic injured tissue at cellular level can cause further brain damage or other organ damage. It's like fire damage in a building resulting in leaking pipes, which causes further damage after the fire has gone out.

**Case Studies:**

***Buenos Aires, Argentina***

In May 2020, Dr Cannellotto, the President of Argentina Association Hyperbaric Medicine and Research, explained in a lecture (in Spanish) published on YouTube the science on why she advocated using hyperbaric oxygenation.[37] Eventually, her clinical trial had to be stopped because the results were so successful. Between July and November 2020, the trial had an interim analysis with 50% of its sample size (40 people were included rather than the intended 80) and it showed a marked benefit of treatment.

By November 2020, when Dr Cannellotto and her colleagues stopped the trial, there was an abundance of clinical case reports and anecdotal evidence showing how hyperbaric oxygenation was being successfully used for relief or remission of the symptoms associated with Long COVID-19. The case report of this Argentinean clinical trial was published and peer-reviewed. It was

---

[37] Dr Mariana Cannellotto, BioBarica's Medical Director, explains and shows evidence on how hyperbaric oxygen therapy can help patients with coronavirus:
https://www.youtube.com/watch?v=OnzZUqPIVZs (2020)

bigger in terms of numbers than the clinical trials reported from Louisiana and China, where (n=5) five people in each trial who were seriously ill were treated and reported on. One must ask, if one was a seriously ill patient in hospital with COVID-19, what would one's answer to this question be: Was a randomised controlled trial necessary for one to want to try hyperbaric oxygenation rather than invasive mechanic ventilation or even invasive oxygenation intubation?

However, before answering the question, one would have been given balanced disclosure (right to know) about the benefits of hyperbaric oxygenation prior to any decision on treatment options. One would have been told the best clinical evidence available at the time. One should assume, for the purpose of answering the question, that one would have been told about the existing clinical experience in the US and China and that, by adding hyperbaric oxygenation sessions each day as necessary to the treatment, there would be no need to put a patient into a coma and give oxygenation using mechanical ventilation. The patients would have been told that the clinical experience to date demonstrates that lives were saved by using this non-invasive hyperbaric oxygenation, which is likely to result in dramatic and rapid recovery of tissue injury at cellular level. One would have been told that this treatment would counter the COVID-19 viral attack on tissue, which was causing one's shortness of breath and other conditions that are caused by the injured or dead cells brought about by hypoxia (lack of oxygen in cells).

What was valuable to convince the medical community was that Dr Cannellotto's trial was a multicentre, open-label randomised controlled trial conducted on 40 people in all. It took place in three hospitals in Buenos Aires, Argentina: '[Patients] with COVID-19 and severe hypoxaemia despite oxygenation supplementation were assigned to receive either hyperbaric oxygenation or the standard treatment for respiratory symptoms for 7 days.' The Cannellotto et al. report stated: 'Results: The trial was stopped after the interim analysis. 40 patients were randomised, 20 in each group.'[38]

The ethical decision to stop was based on the faster recovery rate of those using hyperbaric oxygenation as opposed to the control group. Continuing the trial was determined as unnecessary, as the beneficial results were seen, and the controlled group was being put at greater risk of further complications by being deprived of the benefits of hyperbaric oxygenation. Nevertheless, and unfortunately, the question must be asked: What disclosure was made about the increased risk of complications if one does not have the hyperbaric sessions? Were the already known benefits explained to the patients in the controlled group who did not have hyperbaric oxygenation?

***Coventry and Warwickshire – United Kingdom***

In November 2021, a Dr Tim Robbins and others from the University Hospitals of Coventry and Warwickshire NHS Trust published a report in the National Library of Medicine. In this case, there was no randomisation of patients. Ten consecutive patients admitted with COVID-19 were given 10 sessions of hyperbaric oxygenation over 12 days.

---

[38] Cannellotto et al., 'Hyperbaric oxygen as an adjuvant treatment for patients with COVID-19 severe hypoxaemia: a randomised controlled trial', *Emergency Medical Journal*, Vol. 39, (2022), pp. 88-93. Available online at: https://emj.bmj.com/content/39/2/88?utm_source=adestra&utm_medium=email&utm_campaign=usage&utm_content=monthly&utm_term=1-2022

The results presented 'suggest potential benefits of HBOT', with statistically significant results following 10 sessions.39

**_Tel Aviv - Israel_**

In February 2022, doctors from Israel published a case report called 'Hyperbaric oxygen treatment for long coronavirus disease-19: a case report'. Again, from a legal perspective looking at disclosure law, a judge must determine what treatment a reasonable person in the patient's position would have decided on? What's legally problematic is that the courts could take a patient's rights further. Reading these results, which show the benefit of what is essentially a higher dosage of oxygenation, what would a logical analysis result in? What would be apparent to anyone giving the matter reasonable consideration? All the patients in the trial reports were surviving COVID-19 injury. This new report from Israel was a further report on the best treatment available and were based on this (best) clinical evidence on hand.40

Then, on 12 July 2022, in Israel, a randomised sham control, double-blind clinical trial using 40 hyperbaric oxygenation sessions for post-COVID-19 condition was published. Because a reasonable person in the patient's position must be told about treatment options, a layperson taking a closer look at some of the medical language in the report and the findings should be considered.

---

[39] Robbins, T., Gonevski, M., Clark, C., Baitule, S., Sharma, K., Magar, A., Patel, K., Sankar, S., Kyrou, I., Ali, A. and Randeva, H.S., 'Hyperbaric oxygen therapy for the treatment of long COVID: early evaluation of a highly promising intervention', *Clinical Medicine*, Vol. 21, No. 6, (2021), p. 629

[40] Bhaiyat, A.M., Sasson, E., Wang, Z., Khairy, S., Ginzarly, M., Qureshi, U., Fikree, M. and Efrati, S., 'Hyperbaric oxygen treatment for long coronavirus disease-19: a case report', *Journal of Medical Case Reports*, Vol. 16, No. 1, (February 2022), pp. 1-5

**Tissue Injury at Centre Stage**

Firstly, it's invaluable to note the title of the report because it suggests why hyperbaric oxygenation should be used as a treatment: 'Hyperbaric oxygen therapy improves neurocognitive functions and symptoms of post-COVID condition: randomized controlled trial.' The authors of the study make several references to hypoxic tissue injury being identified and helped. The report references:

a. tissue pathology caused by virus invasion,
b. secondary tissue hypoxia,
c. significant improvement in tissue oxygenation,
d. induced neurogenesis in injured brain tissue,
e. and anti-inflammatory, mitochondrial function restoration.[41]

By the time of this trial, it was widely accepted that the mechanism of COVID-19 can be related to brain tissue pathology caused by virus invasion or indirectly by neuroinflammation and hypercoagulability (tendency to cause blood clots).

**Legally Incorrect Notwithstanding Ethical Approval?**

In a legal scenario, evidence will be given that it's acknowledged and greatly appreciated that these caring professionals rallied around their patients in need and took personal risks of being infected in humankind's fight against the attack of this virus. Evidence can be given that all these

---

[41] Zilberman-Itskovich, S., Catalogna, M., Sasson, E. et al., 'Hyperbaric oxygen therapy improves neurocognitive functions and symptoms of post-COVID condition: randomized controlled trial', *Scientific Reports*, Vol. 12, No. 11252, (2022). Available online at: https://doi.org/10.1038/s41598-022-15565-0

randomised controlled trials obtained ethical approval by the peers of the medical professionals. Nonetheless, an open discussion is needed as to whether these trials were necessary and lawful. The courts have a right to review this type of decision and will take the professionals' expertise into account. However, if one thinks that because one has their peer's ethical approval that the trial is legal, then one is wrong. The law of disclosure and informed consent applies. Were these trials necessary? Can one suggest in the circumstances that any such randomised controlled trials were conducted to convince someone seriously ill with Long COVID-19 for months to try hyperbaric oxygenation for 90 minutes a day for 40 days? The question is: Were the trials conducted for another reason?

Are randomised controlled trials conducted because this is the usual inclusion criteria for Cochranes Reviews? Were they conducted to convince a medical profession who, as a matter of general practice, require randomised controlled trials on humans to be convinced? In a legal scenario, a victim's lawyer will attempt to prove the clinical evidence and scientific evidence. The point is that one will ask: Was the Nuremberg Code considered from a laypersons view? Some have become seriously ill with Long COVID-19 and, in a legal scenario, a victim's lawyer will ask those responsible for discharging the duty of candour as regards adverse events: Were the obligations under the Convention for the Protection of Human Rights and Dignity of the Human and Article 5 on informed consent discussed with the patients? Were people exposed to increased risk of greater complications because they were not given or told in a balanced way the benefits hyperbaric oxygenation had in the human experiments? Will a layperson consider this failure an adverse event and an open disclosure event? This is the legal difficulty about having randomised controlled trials, but in the special circumstances of hyperbaric oxygenation we know more about the benefits to hypoxic (shortage of oxygen) injured tissue based on science. Is it a reasonable logical analysis to say that there were many peer-reviewed publications supporting the use of hyperbaric oxygenation for the injuries now caused by COVID-19 and Long COVID-19 Syndrome prior to the pandemic?

From a legal scenario evaluation, a victim's lawyer will present the significance of anecdotes told by patients or doctors of successful outcomes as a court will do this from the perspective of a reasonable person in the patient's position. Waiting for randomised controlled trials delay the wider use of hyperbaric oxygenation.

**Barriers to use?**

One reverts back to Ireland for a moment. The number of people suffering from Long COVID-19 is a matter of great public concern. Nevertheless, Long COVID-19 on a scientific evidence basis involves hypoxic 'tissue injury' at cellular level. On 6 July 2022, the Irish Parliamentary Health Committee was told by Dr John Lambert, a Consultant in Infectious Diseases in the Mater Hospital, that COVID-19 is causing 'tissue damage'. He also said: 'We have known for 18 months, based on accumulating scientific data, that brain damage is the issue with Long Covid.' Nonetheless, there was no reference at the Parliamentary Health Committee to hyperbaric oxygenation being used for tissue injury or for Long COVID-19. There was no evidence given prior to the pandemic that the Health Service Executive's Hyperbaric Medicine Unit at University Hospital Galway was used for brain damage, for example to reverse tissue injury in the brain of those who had suffered gas embolism, carbon monoxide poisoning, stroke injury, traumatic brain damage or brain damage post-cancer surgery to the brain, or tissue injury in the brain induced by radiation oncology during cancer treatment. Neither was the committee informed that hyperbaric oxygenation was used for other tissue injury, such as that induced by inflammation, infection or arterial insufficiency.

There was no evidence given that patients attending the 'Post Covid Clinic' at the Beacon Hospital in Dublin were being told of the benefits of hyperbaric oxygenation, while patients attending other Health Service Executive post-COVID-19 clinics were not told.[42]

One asks what the barrier was in Ireland and around the globe that stopped the immediate disclosure of and universal use of the known benefits of hyperbaric oxygenation to reverse hypoxic tissue injury at cellular level? The hypothesis advanced here is that it's due to invalid informed consent.

### Commercial Aircraft as Pressure Chambers

When all is said and done, another major conundrum is that this known method of using increased pressure to help save lives from COVID-19 could have been upscaled. If one reads the blog attached to the link below, one will see the lost opportunity.[43] [44] Because

---

[42] 'Effects of Long Covid and Provision of Long Covid Care: Engagement with Dr John Lambert', *Houses of the Oireachtas*, (July 2022). Available online at: https://www.oireachtas.ie/en/debates/debate/joint_committee_on_health/2022-07-06/3/

43 Jason Ford, 'Airliners could have role as Covid-19 hyperbaric oxygen chambers', The Engineer, (2020). Available online at: https://www.theengineer.co.uk/aircraft-hbot-hyperbaric-oxygen-chambers/

The unlikely plan to save COVID-19 patients with planes. In this article: Hyperbaric, Hyperbaric Medicine, coronavirus, Planes, Dr Dan Reynolds, Dr Gerado Bosco, COVID-19, news, gear, tomorrow.

44 Philip B. James, 'Intermittent high dosage oxygen treats COVID-19 infection: the Chinese studies', Medical Gas Research, Vol. 10, No. 2, (2020), p. 63. Available online at: https://pubmed.ncbi.nlm.nih.gov/32541129/

standard commercial aircraft and private jets can be pressurised like a hyperbaric oxygenation chamber and have an over seat oxygen supply for emergency medical use to recover from hypoxia, the treatments could have been used for COVID-19 in every country.

It would have been valuable for the political leaders and the public to consider the lost opportunity in saving lives and our livelihood and freedoms, because hyperbaric oxygenation could have been upscaled. Groups of doctors, scientists and engineers in the US, the UK and in Ireland had objectively and independently advocated upscaling the use of hyperbaric oxygenation. If one thinks that this sounds impossible and too good to be true, these medical and engineer experts will tell you that you are wrong.

Whatever the answer to the conundrum is, we are experiencing a change in the attitudes of patients. Part of the change will be adhering to the law of informed consent. There is a shift of mistrust in some pharmaceuticals by both doctors and patients. There are allegations of commercialism expressed by some of the founding members of the Cochrane Reviews. The financial business world is shifting towards transparency and sustainable business practices. All of this means that balanced disclosure will be taken more seriously. It's valuable to know that valid informed consent makes both the doctor and the patient more powerful in the journey towards good health.

# Chapter Two:

# Hyperbaric Oxygenation - Proof and Explanation

This chapter is a valuable tool to help guide health professionals, be they nurses, podiatrists, nutritional professionals, physiotherapists, speech therapists, dentists, physicians or surgeons, to a legal pathway to obtain a valid informed consent to medical intervention.

An absolutely crucial issue is to understand at the outset that some of these professionals mistakenly think that if they recommend to a client what is standard of care in their clinical practice guidelines, and they practice to this standard, they are safe from being successfully sued.

However, in this case, they are wrong because more information is required for a legitimate informed consent. Unfortunately, many current clinical practice guidelines could be used as verifying evidence to unseat or discredit a defence expert witness. This chapter will help these professionals to avoid unnecessary medico-legal problems.

A further red flag issue for medical professionals is to understand basic lawyer strategies in most legal jurisdictions. Using impeachment or unseating evidence against a defence witness is an experience to be avoided by expert witnesses called by the defence in a law case. The available scientific evidence (the known biological phenomena) is a deciding point to tip the balance in favour of the provable benefits of hyperbaric oxygenation. It's because technology can prove to a court or a jury how a treatment such as hyperbaric oxygenation works. One must take care, as it may feel instinctively wrong for the medical community because of one's training and the medical culture from the United Kingdom. Nonetheless, one must understand (and this can't be over emphasised) that evidence for a reasonable treatment option that might not be good enough quality for the standard of care for a society of healthcare professionals should nevertheless be shared with the patient.

The assumption that hyperbaric oxygenation for disease, tissue injury or cellular hypoxia must be tested in all cases like a typical pharmaceutical drug trial is incorrect. It is valuable to know that a simple factual matrix can be assembled and (n=1) is legally provable.

The universal gas laws such as Boyle's law, Dalton's law, Henry's law and Graham's law already mentioned are universal. They are laws considered as proven. It's helpful to know that these laws cannot be denied in court and that every medical student and medical professional have been trained to understand their application in medicine and are expected to know these laws.

Similarly, proof of arterial insufficiency, ischemia, oedema, hypoxemia and hypoxia is also measurable and easy to explain to a court.

To avoid legal problems, it's my contention that it is imperative to change from traditional thinking about evidence-based medicine and blinded randomised controlled trials. One must think more like a lawyer or a layperson in terms of evidence based on strict science and what results using artificial intelligence without bias would or might determine.

The before and after measurable blood markers are scientific proof for disease severity and/or remission. Inflammatory blood markers and infection blood markers already known are easy to prove in court. From a legal view, it is accepted that video monitors can spectacularly but easily prove results from before and after PET and SPECT images of the healing or new tissue formations in the brain.[45] [46] It's the same with CT scans of the lungs. For heart, urological or gastrointestinal diseases, ulcers, blockages or internal bleeding, the use of wireless inspection endoscopic video recordings can also show the before and after inflammation, tissue injury or healing. It's the same type of proof using dual-energy X-ray for diagnostics in osteoporosis.

For diseases of the eye, such as age-related or diabetic macular degeneration or glaucoma, ocular cicatricial pemphigoid (OCP) and other conditions, the use of before and after ultrasounds or optical coherence tomography or standard eye testing could all be used in a court setting to show benefits of hyperbaric oxygenation.

The use of hyperbaric air has been known for several hundreds of years. With the discovery of oxygen, hyperbaric oxygenation is now delivered in air-filled pressure cabins. Engineers, technicians and undersea workers use them to replicate a diving environment.

---

[45] PET (positron emission tomography)

[46] SPECT (single-photon emission computerised tomography)

The hyperbaric pressure cabins are used on construction sites for tunnels, bridges, harbours, oil rigs and/or on ships, diving, or aviation training. All commercial jet aircraft and spaceships are hyperbaric cabins. Hyperbaric living accommodation for workers is in pressure cabins at oil or gas rigs under the deep oceans using mixed gases. Sometimes thousands of kilometres from land at oil rigs on the other side of the world, technicians or divers can obtain advice from a medical specialist on the other end of a phone. The engineers and technicians discovered that, in addition to decompression sickness, the pressure cabins were good for healing wounds or other tissue injury.

In increasing numbers, hyperbaric cabins are used in people's homes or operated and used by lay people in the community for walk-in elective applications. Even a scuba diver who uses an oxygen rebreather or air when diving is obtaining beneficial hyperbaric oxygenation. It's considered one of the safest non-invasive treatments with few counter-indications or side effects. Doctors began using hyperbaric chambers in hospitals and clinics as treatments or emergency medicine because of positive outcomes in the non-medical industry in the community.

**The Oxygenation Process**

We need oxygen to survive. Unpolluted air is made up of various gases. The air we breathe in is (by volume) 79% nitrogen, 20.95% oxygen, and small amounts of other gases. The air exhaled contains 16% oxygen, so a mouth-to-mouth resuscitation works for an almost-drowned person.

What does a session of hyperbaric oxygenation feel like? In multi-seat chambers, one sits in a cabin that is similar to a private jet aircraft. The pressure experienced on one's ears is similar to one's ears popping on an aircraft when there is a change in pressure. Otherwise, while the pressure impacts one's blood, one doesn't notice the pressure on one's body.

Hyperbaric oxygenation is also called hyperbaric oxygen therapy (HBOT). Hyperbaric oxygenation is the process where a person enters a sealed pressure cabin and breathes in normal air or air with a higher percentage of oxygen at greater than atmospheric pressure. Some countries or languages prefer to call the process high-pressure oxygenation in a pressure cabin. The term 'hyperbaric oxygenation' is used throughout this book for a reason.

Oxygen is the same molecule, even under pressure. The term 'hyperbaric' pressure is misleading as the baric varies with the weather. Professor Philip James, the author of the book *Oxygen and the Brain – The Journey of our Lifetime*, said that even without a chamber, barometric pressure ('baric') can vary by 14% from the lowest pressure recorded to the highest pressure recorded by the Met Office in the UK. In Ireland, the difference in the extremes of barometric pressure is 17.5% from the records published by the Irish Met Office.[47]

Nonetheless, this explains why those people who use oxygen at home or in hospitals as a treatment have a greater benefit on a high atmospheric pressure day. After all, gases dissolve in proportion to the increased pressure. On days that the atmospheric pressure is high, our bodies are subjected to more pressure, and therefore more gases dissolve in our blood and tissue. This alone has a healing effect, as people with arthritis pain

[47] Extreme records for Ireland, including atmospheric pressure, can be found online here: https://www.met.ie/climate/weather-extreme-records. Highest at 1051.9 hPa in Valentia on 28/01/1905 and lowest at 931.2 hPa in Limerick on 28/11/1838.

or migraine will tell you. The weather affects inflammation and pain levels even when breathing air.

Despite the impact of the variation in the atmospheric pressure, which impacted the percentages of dissolved oxygen in the blood and a person's health and even survival, the atmospheric pressure is recorded on patient's charts in some hospitals, however in other hospitals this is not the case.48 This variation in pressure impacts the dosage of oxygen dissolved in the tissue, which was important for COVID-19. Any increase in pressure helps heal the injured tissue, reduces inflammation and helps the body fight infection.

**How Do We Breathe?**

The lungs absorb oxygen from the air we inhale and transfer it to our bloodstream so that it can travel all over the body. Our windpipe (or trachea) carries the air we breathe in and out of our lungs. The windpipe divides into airways called bronchi. These bronchi, in turn, branch into smaller and smaller airways that are too small to be seen by the naked human eye. At the end of the bronchi, there are tiny air sacs called alveoli. This is where the gas exchange happens. The oxygen moves across paper-thin walls to tiny blood vessels called capillaries and then into the blood inside the alveoli. Blood with fresh oxygen is pumped around the body by the heart, where it delivers the oxygen-rich haemoglobin to the different tissue where it maintains healthy organs.

When occluded (restrictive) blood flow occurs due to infection, inflammation, physical injury and trauma, or ageing, the

---

[48] Juul, S., Nielsen, E.E., Feinberg, J., Siddiqui, F., Jørgensen, C.K., Barot, E., Nielsen, N., Bentzer, P., Veroniki, A.A., Thabane, L. and Bu, F., 'Interventions for treatment of COVID-19: A living systematic review with meta-analyses and trial sequential analyses (The LIVING Project)', *PLOS Medicine*, Vol. 17, No. 9, (2020), p. 1003293.

medical problems start. This reduction in oxygenated blood circulation through tissues, joints and organs inevitably causes various issues from injured tissue, to infection, inflammation, hypoxia (deficiency in the amount of oxygen reaching the tissues, degrees of diminishing oxygen levels), to life-threatening conditions and eventual necrosis (the death of cell tissue) and disease. For want of oxygen, the cells suffer. There is arterial insufficiency which can be alleviated by delivering oxygen to the cells.

## Oxygenation Under Pressure

Breathing in oxygen while in the pressure cabin results in haemoglobin saturation. Because the pressure reduces the volume, it takes up less space. The extra oxygen in the plasma reaches into injured tissue or cells at the mitochondrial level that the oxygen might not have otherwise reached. This is producing hyper oxygenated blood and tissue.[49]

This delivery to injured tissue is pivotal as the tissue needs an adequate supply of oxygen to function. Injured tissue naturally attracts oxygen, but the amount that can reach the tissue is restricted due to the injury. Hyperbaric oxygenation increases the supply or the dosage. Indeed, the Nobel Prize for Physiology and Medicine in 2019 was partly for showing how injured tissue attracts oxygen.

With the whole body in the chamber, the process of dissolving more oxygen accelerates and increases the creation of

[49] Ortega, M.A., Fraile-Martinez, O., García-Montero, C., Callejón-Peláez, E., Sáez, M.A., Álvarez-Mon, M.A., García-Honduvilla, N., Monserrat, J., Álvarez-Mon, M., Bujan, J. and Canals, M.L., 'A General Overview on the Hyperbaric Oxygen Therapy: Applications, Mechanisms and Translational Opportunities', *Medicina*, Vol. 57, No. 9, (2021), p. 864. Available online at: https://www.mdpi.com/1648-9144/57/9/864

new blood cells (including stem cells).[50] It also facilitates tissue repair, causes gene therapy, vasculogenesis, angiogenesis and aids in reducing inflammation and pain. Within the oxygenation cabin, there is up to nearly 10 times the regular oxygen supply, occluded blood flow is dramatically reduced, and affected areas are supplied with more oxygenation in the process.

The benefits of hyperbaric oxygenation are directly observable and measurable with old and new technology, from early magnetic resonance imaging (MRI) scans in the 1980s to more advanced imaging now.[51]

It's valuable for the medical community to understand from a legal perspective that the problem for the defence lawyers in failing to use hyperbaric oxygenation is that further evidence is obtainable from the scientific analysis of blood samples taken before and after hyperbaric oxygenation. Increases in stem cell production and other markers are also measurable from the blood samples.

Professor Dominic D'Agostino at the University of South Florida has shown in YouTube talks and medical papers the benefits of using a video camera in cancer and diet research in hyperbaric cabins to look at cells at the level of nanometres using an Atomic Force Microscope.[52] Professor D'Agostino reports that his team use a scanning probe that goes across the surface of the membrane, which observes life down to the level of one atom. This is one billionth of one metre, and Bluetooth is used to relay

---

[50] Thom S.R., Bhopale V.M., Velazquez O.C., et al., 'Stem cell mobilisation by hyperbaric oxygen', *American Journal of Physiology*: *Heart and Circulatory Physiology*, Vol. 290, (2006), p. 1378-86

[51] Buckley, C.J. and Cooper, J.S., 'Hyperbaric Effects On Angiogenesis', StatPearls, (2020). Available online at: https://www.ncbi.nlm.nih.gov/books/NBK482485/

52 Dominic D'Agostino PhD, 'Ketogenic Diet & Hyperbaric Oxygen Therapy', full lecture at Hyperbaric Medical Solutions in Woodbury, NY, (2016)

the images to a computer screen. The video records how the cell and the underlying cellular components change as a function of the oxygenation and a function of hyperbaric oxygenation.

It's of note for medical experts or people who make public comments in the field of cancer research to remember to be careful with coded language about 'no evidence' and the laws on balanced information of available treatments. Cancer is an emotional and fraught area, and I don't want to have a distraction from the central issues in this book, nonetheless treatment options are widening and cancer is not as robust as was considered.[53]

The physical laws of oxygen under pressure and the clinical applications were described in *Textbook of Hyperbaric Medicine* by Kewal K Jain in 1989. This book also deals with the contraindications and complications, such as barotrauma and oxygen toxicity. Another important observation is that, as a result of clinical experience, pressure used in the chamber has changed to lower pressures than previously applied.

---

[53] Poff, A.M., Ari, C., Seyfried, T.N. and D'Agostino, D.P., 'The ketogenic diet and hyperbaric oxygen therapy prolong survival in mice with systemic metastatic cancer', *PLOS One*, Vol. 8, No. 6, (2013), p. 65522

# Chapter Three:

# Law and Ethics are Changing Medical Practice

The law is sometimes unpredictable. The most important message in this chapter is to be aware that expert medical evidence of what is approved medical practice is not determinative when it comes to what must be disclosed to a patient about treatment options. What a medical professional must disclose is governed by law and current common medical practices need to make changes to comply with the law.

New interpretations of the law push out the boundaries of what is required in medical practice. The law cases in this chapter will show that it's a further legal problem for medical professionals because the client must decide on the medical interventions, however, only after all reasonable treatment options have been disclosed in a balanced way. What's reasonable in law is the layperson's view as determined by the court, but this is known as the reasonable person test.

This chapter is a tool to help medical professionals deal with the legal problems in the pathways to obtain a legally required, valid informed consent to medical intervention. It's about disclosure and the legal cases in the chapter will show that this means a balanced discussion about the available forms of treatment to undergo. It's best regarded as a customer making choices due to a legal right. This may be easily understood by a contrasting scenario. A service provider such as an airline company doesn't have to disclose to a customer about an alternative flight option with a different airline. However, a medical professional does, as one must take reasonable care to inform patients or make full disclosure of all reasonable treatment options as part of the duty of care. It will be discussed later whereby a medical professional has to turn away business if one cannot provide a particular treatment or one is using inferior diagnostic or treatment equipment, and this is dangerously problematic.

It's vital for all health professionals to understand that, as a result of the UK Supreme Court's radical change in 2015 in the interpretation of the law, an equal shift in one's practice of medicine is required. The legal relationship between the clinician and the patient has changed. This change may cause major legal problems for those in the practice of medicine in the UK. The UK's law courts transferred the decision making to a patient-focused module. It took 41 years for the UK to follow the pathway of the US and 15 years to follow Ireland.

The legal problem for the UK medical community is that the interpretation of the law of disclosure and informed consent has changed overnight. The UK Supreme Court stated in 2015 that its earlier decisions on the issue were wrongly decided. What's unfair is that a medical culture is slower to adapt and not easy to change. A legacy of this is that the format of the clinical practice guidelines has not changed to help doctors keep up with the legal changes.

What is legally problematic and frustrating for doctors is that the changing meaning of legal disclosure and the changing meaning of legal consent in the pathway to informed consent is unpredictable.

## US Case Law

### *Sponenburgh v. County of Wayne*

This is a case in which doctors had to face difficulties and it shows the medical community's legal problems. The victim was awarded $3.08 million compensation, partly due to the failure to use face mask oxygenation and the hyperbaric oxygenation facility in the hospital for carbon monoxide poisoning.54 Brian Sponenburgh, a 16-year-old boy, suffered a permanent brain injury due to carbon monoxide poisoning in 1968. The case was heard in 1977 with an appeal ruling in 1981. Because the victim won, the American Medical Association notified *all* doctors about the case's outcome. Hyperbaric oxygenation is now used in emergency medicine for carbon monoxide poisoning globally. Nonetheless, it is wise to look ahead at a red flag issue because hyperbaric oxygenation is underused in some countries for other poisoning events, including drug overdose.

This Sponenburgh type of case can become problematic for doctors. Knowing about this case is of value nonetheless as a guideline to a medical professional's practice because it shows legal problems. After all, lawyers are allowed to use 'impeachment evidence' to deflect or unseat defence witnesses.

---

[54] *Sponenburgh v. Wayne County*, 106 Mich. App. 628, 308 N.W.2d 589 (Mich. Ct. App. 1981). Available online at:

https://casetext.com/case/sponenburgh-v-wayne-county?

Being attacked on cross-examination with impeachment evidence is a red flag, mainly because no doctor wants it to happen.

It's valuable to know about this tactic because unsuspecting defence expert witnesses could find their reputation under attack in a matter of minutes. Because of professional collegiality, the victim's witnesses might not be so forthcoming, so impeachment evidence is a tactic to show inconsistencies and contradictions in the defence. In the manoeuvre of unseating someone, any out-of-court statements by defence witnesses are becoming easier to find because of YouTube, Twitter, LinkedIn and other social media. In cross-examination, the utterances can be used against a party's interest and damage the defence contended for.

The defendants in the Sponenburgh case ran into legal problems with their defence contended for as regards hyperbaric oxygenation. One hospital doctor claimed that hyperbaric oxygenation was a 'fad'. A defence witness said that the chamber was (only) purchased for the purpose of 'research and investigation'. Another witness for the defence stated that it was not 'the standard of care' in 1968 to use hyperbaric oxygenation for carbon monoxide poisoning and therefore claimed that it was not malpractice. However, one will see later that this is not a defence to the law of disclosure and informed consent. There were other malpractice issues as well.

The victim's lawyers used impeachment evidence such as hospital records, which showed another patient with severe carbon monoxide poisoning was treated with hyperbaric oxygenation in the same hospital and recovered. Evidence of a local newspaper article and a photograph of a new chamber with a caption saying that it could be used to treat 'victims of poison' was also used to unseat the defence witnesses.

The victim's lawyer, using further impeachment evidence according to the judgment of the Court of Appeal, read the following hearsay excerpt from a 1976 article in the British Medical Journal: 'Emergency treatment of a patient suspected of carbon monoxide poisoning includes removal of the victim from the source of poisoning, administration of 100 per cent oxygen by tight-fitting face mask and immediate transportation to a hospital where hyperbaric treatment is available.'

What is further legally problematic for the medical community is that lawyers can now use evidence on injured tissue level in brain injury cases because of the ability SPECT images have to show remission in tissue injury in cerebral anomalies. These anomalies can be similar to tissue injury in carbon monoxide poisoning brain injury anomalies.

In any future legal scenario, it's valuable for neurologists to understand that victims' lawyers are likely to point out the tissue injury that resulted in Brian Sponenburgh suffering from certain neurological abnormalities, which were spastic paralysis of his body, loss of vision, inability to communicate, inability to walk without external support, and loss of coordination in his limbs, hands and feet.

In a legal scenario dealing especially with concussion, traumatic brain injury or dementia, the lawyers for sports participants such as boxers, National Football League (NFL) players, rugby players and/or war veterans will find it easy to prove that hyperbaric oxygenation should have been explained to patients as part of the pathway for obtaining informed consent.

In addition, victims' lawyers could use reported medical research on successful neurological outcomes. The powerful point is to consider that the function of a judge or a jury is to determine if a reasonable person in the patient's position would consider the information significant. Simple examples of successful outcomes would be the research carried out by Dr Shai Efrati in Israel, or new results from the Aviv Clinics in Florida and Dubai of hyperbaric oxygenation on traumatic brain injury, aging or using hyperbaric oxygenation for dementia.[55]

Similar technology (SPECT image) has been used by Dr Paul Harch and Dr Edward Fogarty to show a single case (n=1) successful outcome for Alzheimer's disease.[56] A case in point is that Bruce Willis, the American actor, was recently diagnosed with Aphasia, which is a neurological or brain disorder. This is another brain hypoxic tissue injury at cellular level and hyperbaric oxygenation is known to help.[57] Unfortunately, the lack of publicity around hyperbaric oxygenation being used as a treatment option for Aphasia may be a direct result of the article on the Food and Drug Administration website called 'Don't be Misled', which has brain injury in the 'don't be misled' list.

My message is that attack must be the best form of defence here when doctors are accused of misleading others or giving false hope. On the contrary, giving balanced disclosure is fulfilling a legal obligation to avoid an invalid informed consent before a medical intervention.

---

[55] Tal, S., Hadanny, A., Berkovitz, N., Sasson, E., Ben-Jacob, E. and Efrati, S., 'Hyperbaric oxygen may induce angiogenesis in patients suffering from prolonged post-concussion syndrome due to traumatic brain injury', *Restorative Neurology and Neuroscience*, Vol. 33, No. 6, (2015), pp. 943-51

[56] Harch, P.G. and Fogarty, E.F., 'Hyperbaric oxygen therapy for Alzheimer's dementia with positron emission tomography imaging: a case report', *Medical Gas Research*, Vol. 8, No. 4, (2018), p. 181

[57] 'Aphasia Awareness and treating with HBOT.' More information can be sourced online here: https://communityhyperbaric.com/aphasia-and-hbot/

***Canterbury v Spence***

This United States case was the beginning of a recurring problem for the medical community about the patient's 'right to know', called 'disclosure' in other legal jurisdictions. The case was affirmation of the importance of the right to balanced disclosure of information material to the decision making prior to medical professionals obtaining a valid informed consent. The law of informed consent was thereby dramatically changed. Medical malpractice law was reshaped in *Canterbury v Spence* in 1972 as the court set out the general principle.[58] The court explained that: 'A physician is under a duty to treat his patient skilfully, but proficiency in diagnosis and therapy is not the full measure of his responsibility. The cases demonstrate that the physician is under an obligation to communicate specific information to the patient when the exigencies of reasonable care call for it.'

The court determined that the patient has 'a right to know of all material risks associated with a proposed form of treatment, the reasonable alternatives and that the patient can choose which treatment to pursue'. One will see later that the UK and Irish courts also used the expression 'reasonable alternatives' and this means possible alternative treatments that are not the medical professionals' normal recommended treatment. In this radical case, the trial court allowed the determination of the issue of adequate disclosure and informed consent to go to the jury without the need for expert evidence.

Unfortunately for the medical community, there are further problematic issues for failure to disclose risk. The court said: 'Many of the issues typically involved in nondisclosure cases do

---

[58] *Canterbury v. Spence*, 464 F.2d 772 (D.C. Cir. 1972)

not reside peculiarly within the medical domain. Lay witness testimony can competently establish a physician's failure to disclose particular risk information, the patient's lack of knowledge of the risk, and the adverse consequences following the treatment.'[12]

This change occurred against a background of what was described by the trial judge as a possible 'conspiracy of silence' where local doctors, most likely due to collegiality, would not testify against a fellow doctor. Nonetheless, the court ruled that an expert was not needed, and the case proceeded without a doctor as an expert witness. Without an expert witness, the jury could decide the standard of information required for informed consent. The court ruled on 'what a reasonable patient would want to know' prior to making a decision on the treatment options. Dr Spence won, as the jury was satisfied that he gave the patient sufficient information for the patient to decide on the treatment.

### *The T.J. Hooper Case*

***'It's negligent even if a whole calling lags behind.'***

Although the subject of this book is on informed consent and the necessary disclosure for this consent to be valid, it's necessary to highlight an aspect of medical negligence law. The courts have reluctance to interfere with the standard of care or what is normal and do not generally tell the medical professionals what to do. However, an American appeal court reserved the right to have oversight of what is standard medical practice. In Ireland, in a medical negligence case of *Dunne v The National Maternity Hospital* involving the birth of twins, the court took a similar practical observation: that medical treatment may be negligent, even if it accords with 'general and approved practice', and that practice has defects that would be apparent to anyone giving the matter reasonable consideration.[59] In the UK, a similar approach to the *T.J. Hooper* and *Dunne* cases is followed. In *Montgomery v Lanarkshire Health Board*, the court said: 'notwithstanding the views of medical experts, the court may conclude that their opinion is incapable of withstanding logical analysis.'[60]

It is of interest to note that the *British Medical Journal* has frequently referenced articles about the law case of The *T.J. Hooper*, which is a case about a sea captain's failure to have a radio onboard and to use this radio for listening to weather forecasts in 1932. An American court held that an industry's general custom does not dictate the standard of care. It is for the court to decide what is required of the parties.[61]

The logical analysis in *The T.J. Hooper* judgment has lasted the test of time. It was held that the court reserves the right to apply a common sense or a common prudence approach, and it's not a defence if almost all in the profession are making the same mistake. This is referenced here to help the medical community understand why change is needed in thinking. The science supporting hyperbaric oxygenation medicine and the law of informed consent will be problematic in defending doctors' conduct who are unwilling to change, as a common-sense approach will be taken. The judge said: 'In most cases, reasonable

---

[59] Dunne [an infant] v The National Maternity Hospital, WJSC-SC, 165, (1989)

[60] Montgomery v Lanarkshire Health Board and Intervener, General Medical Council, GWD 10-179, (2015). Available online at: https://www.bailii.org/uk/cases/UKSC/2015/11.html

[61] *The T.J. Hooper*, 60 F:2d 737 (2d Cir.), cert. denied, 287 U.S. 662, (1932)

prudence is, in fact, common prudence; but strictly, it is never its measure; a whole calling may have unduly lagged in the adoption of new and available devices.'

In the context of hyperbaric oxygenation, it may be argued using the *Dunne* case, the *Montgomery* case and the *Hooper* case, that a hospital has lagged behind and is negligent by not having or using a hyperbaric chamber.[62] [63] In any event, if a doctor or nurse knows their hospital does not have up-to-date equipment and that another hospital has better equipment, the law of disclosure and informed consent requires that this is disclosed. Otherwise, it's an invalid informed consent.

**TreatNow and Army Veterans**

The legal problems surrounding the law of informed consent and the medical interventions for US veterans who have suffered traumatic brain injury are valuable to examine. Serious illness, chronic pain, migraine or chronic medical conditions are well documented to be a factor or cause of suicide. Traumatic head injury is also documented to be a factor or cause of suicide. Because of the urgency needed to prevent suicides, as shown in the TreatNow website, the US organisation TreatNow advocates using the law of informed consent to medical intervention to quickly establish hyperbaric oxygenation as primary care for brain injury.[64]

---

[62] Ibid., Sponenburgh v. Wayne County (1981)

[63] See Csiszar, A., Gautam, T., Sosnowska, D., Tarantini, S., Banki, E., Tucsek, Z., et al., 'Caloric Restriction Confers Persistent anti-oxidative, Pro-angiogenic, and anti-inflammatory Effects and Promotes anti-aging miRNA Expression Profile in Cerebromicrovascular Endothelial Cells of aged Rats', Am. J. Physiology-Heart Circulatory Physiol, Vol. 307, (2014), pp. 292–306

[64] TreatNOW on their homepage: 'The VA and DOD spend billions looking for symptom-management solutions, but don't provide veterans with "informed consent" about safe and effective treatments on the market' (2021). Available online at: https://treatnow.org/

The spokesperson for the TreatNow organisation (Dr Robert L Beckman, PhD) said it is a citizen's response to the army veterans' suicide epidemic.[65] [66] In addition to suicides, veterans living with serious pain are part of the opioid epidemic. TreatNow has been established to try and make the States or public health pay for hyperbaric oxygenation for these people suffering from traumatic brain injury (TBI) and related conditions.

This, unfortunately, raises the question as to why all doctors have not at least been telling the patient about hyperbaric oxygenation. Advocates for hyperbaric oxygenation in the US contend that it's difficult to comprehend any consent to the medical intervention being valid without being told about hyperbaric oxygenation.

The legal problem for lawyers defending clinicians is that the *Sponenburgh* and the *Canterbury v Spence* law cases open the door for successful litigation. Also, the legal proofs are now easier to prove with the technological advances since Brian Sponenburgh won his case in the lower court and on appeal. It's not going to be too difficult in predicting the outcomes of law cases based on the law of disclosure and informed consent as it will be a judge deciding on what is reasonable.

The red flag issue is that in a legal scenario, it's a judge or a jury who will be determining if a reasonable person in the patient's position would have decided to use the hyperbaric oxygenation option. Staff or clients who have experience with hyperbaric oxygenation services can provide evidence of the fact that customers (clients) opted for the hyperbaric oxygenation

---

[65] Ibid.

[66] Carol Giacomo, 'Suicide Has Been Deadlier Than Combat for the Military', *New York Times*, (2019). Available online at: https://www.nytimes.com/2019/11/01/opinion/military-suicides.html

option, based on the known scientific evidence or anecdotal evidence, and were not influenced by the shortage of blinded randomised controlled trials.

Suppose a medical professional does not inform a war veteran about the known benefits of hyperbaric oxygenation and proceeds with a medical intervention; in that case, the doctor is understandably at risk that the veteran or their personal representatives in the case of suicide will take successful legal action. Hyperbaric oxygenation is not approved by the Food and Drug Administration for brain injury. Nevertheless, if the clinician thinks that because it's not approved this makes it a defence to a claim for failing to make balanced disclosure of the risks involved in not using hyperbaric oxygenation as a treatment option for brain injury, again, in this case, it is not correct. There are many case reports showing the benefits, especially from Tel Aviv.[67]

## UK Case Law

The law in the UK in 2015 dramatically changed the legal pathway to obtain a valid informed consent to any medical intervention. In fact, the Supreme Court said that the House of Lords' earlier decision about disclosure in 1957 was wrong and incorrectly decided. This change in the interpretation of the law occurred because of the case of a Nadine Montgomery and her

---

[67] Three case report examples are (1) Balasubramanian et al., 'Integrative Role of Hyperbaric Oxygen Therapy on Healthspan, Age-Related Vascular Cognitive Impairment, and Dementia', (2021) and

(2) J Neurotrauma (Feb 2018), Vol. 35, No. 4, pp. 623–629. PMCID: PMC6909681, PMID: 29132229

'Hyperbaric Oxygen Therapy in the Treatment of Acute Severe Traumatic Brain Injury: A Systematic Review',and

(3) Samuel Daly,1,,2 Maxwell Thorpe,1 Sarah Rockswold,3 Molly Hubbard,1,,4 Thomas Bergman,1,,4 Uzma Samadani,1,,4 and Gaylan Rockswold corresponding author1,,4

child who suffered brain damage at birth. Ms Montgomery was not given information about a caesarean section as an option, so the court found that she gave an invalid informed consent.

Nonetheless, it's a legal issue to understand. Necessary adjustments are needed such as changing clinical practice guidelines, as many have not followed the radical legal change.

Again, it's useful to pause here and look forward to other possibilities for change for the better. It took the law courts to change medical practice for childbirth, nonetheless, based on a changed interpretation of the law of consent to medical intervention. This change in the law is only because of the story of Nadine Montgomery, who sued the Lanarkshire Health Board because her doctors did not obtain informed consent.[68] She was not told about a caesarean section as an option because the medical professionals said they feared that she and other women might have decided to have this intervention.

Nadine Montgomery was a woman of small stature with diabetes, whose child was born with serious and permanent disabilities resulting from a brain injury at birth. Because Ms Montgomery's obstetrician had not warned her of the risk of shoulder dystocia, where the baby's shoulder can be bigger than the head and get stuck during vaginal delivery, the hospital lost in the Supreme Court. However, the hospital won in the Scottish High Court and the Scottish Court of Appeal because a reasonable body of professional opinion supported not telling Ms Montgomery. The hospital won in the lower courts because the doctors were allowed to 'know better' than the patient and were legally allowed to decide for the patient. The Supreme Court

---

[68] *Montgomery v Lanarkshire Health Board* and *Intervener*, General Medical Council, (GWD 10-179, 2015). Available online at: https://www.bailii.org/uk/cases/UKSC/2015/11.html

overturned the lower courts' decisions. The trial and two appeals were hard-fought by the doctors and the hospital, despite changes in the General Medical Council's documents about informed consent being a basic model of partnership between patient and doctor. It could be said that the law caught up with the guidelines.

Nevertheless, problematically for doctors, years of clinical practice and culture that was part of the law had to be changed overnight in the UK. The foundational legal principle known as the 'doctor knows best' principle was reversed, and the patient became the decision-maker on treatment options.

It's now dangerous to practice medicine if one does not understand the story about the *Bolam* case. This was the original case to establish the legal principle known as the 'doctor knows best' principle. Mr John Bolam is famous in medical law because he lost his medical negligence case, which has now dramatically been found to have been wrongly decided.

The story began in 1954, when Mr Bolam voluntarily went into a psychiatric hospital suffering from depression. He had electro-convulsive therapy (ECT). The claim was that he was thrown from a couch by the electric current and fell violently onto the floor. He had 'stove-in' fractures of the sockets of both hip bones and had to use a wheelchair for the rest of his life. Mr Bolam sued for damages for medical negligence.

His expert medical witnesses said that Mr Bolam should have been sedated, strapped down and adequately informed of the risk involved before agreeing to the procedure. People may be shocked to learn why the defendants in the case were successful. They won because they argued that if Mr Bolam had been informed about the dangers of the electric shock treatment, he might have refused the treatment. The impact of the case was that the doctors knew best and, if he had been informed of the dangers, this could have caused him to refuse the treatment and suffer further harm. From this case on, all a medical professional had to do was find colleagues who would give evidence from a reasonable body of expert opinion that what was done was an acceptable practice.

In the UK, from then on, it did not matter that those other doctors disagreed. In the *Montgomery* case, because the Supreme Court said that the Bolam case was wrongly decided, this is problematic for doctors and hospitals since the current decision applies retrospectively.

However, new UK General Medical Council guidelines have been changed several times since the *Montgomery* case started, with the most recent being published in September 2020. The guidelines, similar to earlier guidelines, say: 'The exchange of information between doctor and patient is central to good decision making.' The guidelines say that doctors must refer to options or reasonable alternatives. This new reference to the obligation of the doctor to articulate reasonable alternatives is critical. It states: 'Doctors must try to find out what matters to patients so they can share relevant information about the benefits and harms of proposed options and reasonable alternatives, including the option to take no action.' Unfortunately, the guidelines do not specifically mention the *Montgomery* case that changed the law for the medical community and do not explain the medico-legal problems due to invalid informed consent.[69]

---

[69] Ethical guidance for doctors, available online at: https://www.gmc-uk.org/ethical-guidance/ethical-guidance-for-doctors

It is crucial in almost every jurisdiction for the medical community to remember the next two sentences from the new UK Supreme Court interpretation of the law for the standard to be followed to obtain informed consent. The sentences are: 'The doctor is therefore under a duty to take reasonable care to ensure that the patient is aware of any material risks involved in any recommended treatment and of any reasonable alternative or variant treatments. The doctor cannot form an objective, "medical" view of these matters, and is therefore not in a position to take the "right" decision as a matter of clinical judgment.'

A red flag dangerous trap is to be complacent, as it's a judge or a jury who decides what is reasonable. No matter what area of practice one is in, reasonable care is making oneself aware of what alternative options there are. A further tactic for the victim's lawyer would be to cross-examine the defendant doctor on what reasonable treatment options one has discussed before now with other patients. One can see in the *Montgomery* case that a responsible body of medical opinion, being the witnesses called by the defence, did not approve of the alternative, but this did not matter.

In addition, and this is vital to remember in order to avoid invalidating an informed consent, is that doctors can have their different opinions about, say, one case report (n=1) or some other clinical matter. Still, the law requires good disclosure and for options to be explained in a balanced way.

Remembering the uncertain outcome in legal cases mentioned earlier, it's invaluable to know for improving medical practice of the welfare of the patient and, from a legal perspective, that hyperbaric oxygenation has successfully been used on new-borns with brain injury with good results.[70]

The result in the *Sponenburgh v. Wayne County* case for other medical indications is likely to be repeated. This dangerous scenario will be recurring unless there is a change in the editorial policy of both the Cochrane Reviews and clinical practice guidelines which are discussed later.

## Irish Legal Case Law

The change in the interpretation of the legal relationship between client and clinician did not happen overnight. It resulted from a gradual shift over many years in the case law and the culture of medicine to a more collaborative and client-focused approach.

The 'doctor knows best' attitude is noticeable in the language of the judges in earlier cases. In *Daniels v Heskin*, the medical paternalism of the 1950s is evident.[71] The court held that doctors were free to disclose or withhold information.

---

[70] Xiong, T., Li, H., Zhao, J., Qu, Y., Mu, D., Dong, W. and Wu, T., 'Hyperbaric oxygen for term newborns with hypoxic ischaemic encephalopathy', *The Cochrane Database of Systematic Reviews*, Vol. 3, (2019)

Wei, L., Wang, J., Cao, Y., Ren, Q., Zhao, L., Li, X. and Wang, J., 'Hyperbaric oxygenation promotes neural stem cell proliferation and protects the learning and memory ability in neonatal hypoxic-ischemic brain damag', *International journal of clinical and experimental pathology*, Vol. 8 No. 2, (2015) p. 1752

Memar, M.Y., Yekani, M., Alizadeh, N. and Baghi, H.B., 'Hyperbaric oxygen therapy: Antimicrobial mechanisms and clinical application for infections', *Biomedicine & Pharmacotherapy*, Vol. 109, (2019), pp. 440-47

Mirasoglu, B., Cetin, H., Akgun, S.O. and Aktas, S., 'Hyperbaric oxygen treatment for intrauterine limb ischaemia: a newborn in the chamber', *Diving and Hyperbaric Medicine*, Vol. 51, No. 2, (2021), pp. 220-23

[71] [1954] I.R. 73 Maguire CJ

### *Geoghegan v Harris*

Despite this gradual change, Ireland was 15 years ahead of the UK in making a change in the interpretation of the law. Still, it may be that the medical community in Ireland followed the medical community in the UK because medical societies overlap.

Nonetheless, the law and the medical community's attitudes have since moved on. In the case of *Geoghegan v Harris*, the High Court in the year 2000 held that the consent process was negligent, as Dr Harris did not obtain the informed consent of Mr Geoghegan, as the risk of chronic pain was a known potential complication and was not sufficiently disclosed.[72] A warning of the risk was required. The lack of a valid consent process was indicative of negligence. In the judgment, Judge Nicholas Kearns affirmed the right of the court to take priority over the views or opinion evidence of medical experts about the treatment options and the legal test about what should be explained. He called this the reasonable person test, so the judge had to consider what the reasonable person in the patient's position would want to be told. Seven years later, this case and law was affirmed in the Irish Supreme Court.[73] The American case of *Canterbury v Spence* was referenced and followed.

---

[72] *Geoghegan v Harris* [2000] 3 IR 536. Seven years later this was affirmed in the Irish Supreme Court in Fitzpatrick v White [2007] IESC 51

[73] Fitzpatrick v White [2007] IESC 51

***Fitzpatrick v K***

The second key strand of informed consent is whether the client has been adequately informed of the alternative or variant treatments. In *Fitzpatrick v K*, the Irish court clarified in 2008 that for the consent to be legitimate, the patient must have been allowed to consider the treatment information, particularly 'the alternative choices and the likely outcomes, in the balance in arriving at a decision'.[74]

There is a growing community of patients, patient advocates, healthcare providers, healthcare indemnity insurers and lawyers looking for ways to avoid medical negligence litigation. This tool in law and ethics to avoid liability for injury is obtaining valid informed consent to medical intervention. It allows the patient to be empowered to take the risk knowingly and, therefore, willingly.

---

[74] Fitzpatrick v FK and another [2008] IEHC 104, [2009] 2 IR 7

# Chapter Four:

# Why do Leading Countries around the Globe Differ in Healthcare Treatments Offered?

If scientific evidence was followed in both Japan and the US, one would expect a convergence of similar offerings for treating the same diseases or injuries, but this is not the case. Unfortunately, with hyperbaric oxygenation, the divergence has caused people to miss treatment opportunities in healthcare that increased their risk of adverse medical events and exposed people to avoidable consequences.

Examples of divergences in treatments are that Japan uses hyperbaric oxygenation to treat neurological anomalies, such as severe traumatic brain injury and spinal nerve disorder. One has picked this example as the risk of not using hyperbaric oxygenation would likely cause grave consequences for the patient and would affect up to 15% of the population. It's covered by national health insurance and is in general an approved practice in Japan, but the Food and Drug Administration has not approved these indications.[75]

In the same way, Japan also uses hyperbaric oxygenation as a concurrent treatment with chemotherapy and radiation oncology, but the Food and Drug Administration has not approved it.[76] [77] It's the same disparity of care for treating non-union open tibial fracture between Japan and the Food and Drug Administration. This latter medical condition will be discussed in connection with the Cochrane Reviews to suggest why this discrepancy is happening. A disparity is seen when the Food and Drug Administration may be asking for a randomised controlled trial for using hyperbaric oxygenation for a disease or injury prior to approval, whereas the opposite comes about in other parts of the globe due to the faithful adherence to ethical considerations in the Nuremberg Code.

**European Union Cross-Border Healthcare Directive**

All of the indications for hyperbaric oxygenation available in Japan are available in Europe free of charge. One question in the litigation for informed consent was: Would the patient, if told about a treatment option, have taken the treatment? In Ireland, each public hospital consultant can refer public patients to the Irish state-owned Hyperbaric Medicine Unit and this service is free. If there is no availability, the patient can be referred to any other clinic in the European Union under the EU Cross-Border Directive, and the Irish State pays the other member state.

---

[75] Jain, Kewel K., *Textbook of Hyperbaric Medicine* (6th Edition), NY, Springer, (2017)

76 See list of indication for Japan in Chapter Seven.

77 List of indications – UHMS Indications, available online at: https://www.uhms.org/images/UHMS-Reference-Material.pdf

By this stage in this book, one knows that reasonable care must be taken to discuss risks and treatment options. Nevertheless, taking reasonable care to disclose treatment options is not confined to what is available in the country the clinician is practicing in. Unfortunately, unseating evidence against the interest of a defendant is the amount of information in medical journals about the EU Cross-Border Healthcare Directive.

In Europe, under the Directive, entitled people (generally EU citizens) can access healthcare in other EU or EEA member states.[78] Under the Directive, the patient can receive any medicinal product or equipment authorised in the member state of treatment even if the medicinal product or equipment is not authorised in the patient's member state of origin.

**What Is Different as Regards the Pathways for Educating Both Doctors and Patients?**

A Cochrane Reviews report is a useful example to gain some insight as to why people in the US are behind Japan in using hyperbaric oxygenation. To help the Cochrane Reviews editors, they are asked to obtain independent legal advice personally as regards their clinical practice and for the legal issues as regards defects with the editorial policy concerning oxygenation. If the court determines that the general and approved practice is unlawful, then the standard rule of allowing professionals to set their own standards does not apply. However, this book is about disclosure and invalid informed consent.

[78] Directive 2011/24/EU of the European Parliament and of the Council of 9 March 2011 on the application of patients' rights in cross-border healthcare.

The title of the chosen review is: 'Hyperbaric oxygen therapy for promoting fracture healing and treating fracture non-union' (2012).[79] What's said about the Cochrane Reviews in this discussion is focused on hyperbaric oxygenation only and it is important for this analysis. One will see that the Cochrane Reviews' authors seek empirical data without taking into account the scientific information already there to prove that tissue will suffer hypoxic tissue injury at the cellular level and die for want of oxygen. It's helpful in this discussion about the editorial formula of the Cochrane Reviews to understand the law. One must understand, as editors, that the patient's decision should not depend solely on the medical professionals' considerations and how approval comes about for general treatment practice and recommendations.

It's seen here that a call in the review for 'good quality clinical trials' in reality means Cochrane Reviews' requirement for randomised controlled trials on humans if the information is to be captured by the inclusion criteria. This is a step on the way to approval for general practice. Nevertheless, with this narrow focus, the significance attached by the Cochrane Reviews to experiments with humans is nonetheless in imminent danger of being profoundly conflicted with law and ethics. My insider's view as a lawyer and someone with an understanding of hyperbaric oxygenation has helped me see that, because modern technology can indisputably prove biological phenomena, the Cochrane Reviews' authors in their true mission are failing the medical professionals. This mission is to educate medical professionals so they can in turn help patients make informed decisions based on

---

[79] Bennett, M.H., Stanford, R.E. and Turner, R., 'Hyperbaric oxygen therapy for promoting fracture healing and treating fracture non-union', *Cochrane Database of Systematic Reviews*, (2012)

evidence in healthcare. The randomisation of humans is unnecessary and unethical because of the gas laws, known biological phenomena of hyperbaric oxygenation and alternative scientific observation methods.

The aim here, however, is to suggest changes needed as to how Cochrane Reviews might see their defective methodology and how one could help medical professionals practice within the law, as they must make balanced disclosure to obtain a valid informed consent to medical intervention. For clarity, this disclosure and consent is a different legal consideration from the ordinary consideration of medical negligence as regards standards for diagnosis and treatment that the professionals set for themselves. Nevertheless, the defects regarding oxygenation and the failure to embrace scientific evidence could possibly result in the court bringing about change to medical practice that is general and approved. It's a possible red flag warning to highlight again the inherent defects in general practice already disclosed in the *T.J. Hooper* case in the US, the *Montgomery* case in the UK and the *Dunne* case in Ireland. This red flag warning also applies to defects in the way the Food and Drug Administration makes decisions that influence the standards of care in the US and beyond.

It's worth giving the relevant quote from the *Dunne* case, as the court explained that: 'If a medical practitioner charged with negligence defends his conduct by establishing that he followed a practice which was general, and which was approved of by his colleagues of similar specialisation and skill, he cannot escape liability if in reply the plaintiff establishes that such practice has inherent defects which ought to be obvious to any person giving the matter due consideration.'[80]

One attempts here to give a summary of an insider's insight as a lawyer and as a reasonable layperson in the patient's position. The discussion is back to confining one's argument to disclosure and invalid informed consent. As explained earlier, I had a fractured pelvis in 2015 and extensive trauma. I was told by my UK doctors that not all the doctors agreed with the sequelae; however, the consensus was that I would be in a wheelchair for 13 weeks before I could support weight on my legs and pelvis. On my return to Ireland, the Irish professor of orthopaedic surgery looking after me relied on and monitored my periodic X-rays. Travelling from either St James's Hospital or a rehabilitation centre, I had daily sessions of private hyperbaric oxygenation in Dublin over four weeks. When the surgeon considered my final X-ray report, he gave me a date six weeks earlier than predicted that my legs and pelvis could support my weight. This meant that one spent much less time confined to a wheelchair as well as other obvious benefits.

Let's say for example, a person had a non-union open tibial fracture. There was ischaemia, arterial insufficiency and poor tissue viability as a result of the trauma that caused the fracture. This led to complications such as severe pain, infection, continued non-union and eventual amputation. The patient was not told about hyperbaric oxygenation and the material risk to amputation if this treatment option was not used and takes legal action against the hospital based on the law of disclosure and

---

[80] Dunne [an infant] v The National Maternity Hospital, WJSC-SC, 165, (1989) I.R. 91 Page 109 (Electronic reference to the paragraph is available in Ruth Morrissey v Ireland at: https://www.bailii.org/ie/cases/IESC/2020/2020IESC6_0.html

informed consent. His orthopaedic surgeon is Dr A. The lawyer defending the conduct of Dr A and the hospital in this scenario will have a difficult time defending a failure to disclose the known benefits of hyperbaric oxygenation. In a legal scenario, let's consider the four cumulative requirements in chapter one:

a) One can prove that there is an extra risk to the limb in not using the alternative treatment option, which is hyperbaric oxygenation.
b) Hyperbaric oxygenation is material in the care of the hypoxic tissue injury at cellular level and the risk and alternative was not explained.
c) It's a judge who will determine if the reasonable person in the patient's position was given balanced disclosure about hyperbaric oxygenation; the patient would have considered it material and it would have been used.
d) In a legal scenario for assessing evidence, it's the balance of probabilities that are used to determine if there would have been a materially better outcome for the limb.

If Cochrane Reviews fail to help medical professionals practice within the law of disclosure and informed consent, in this case, it's inappropriate to medical practice and dangerous for Dr A to rely on in the above scenario.

A lawyer for a victim could call a witness who was a patient in a similar situation to Dr A's patient. However, this patient can tell the court that one was informed about hyperbaric oxygenation to promote fracture healing. A narrative could be given why the person used hyperbaric oxygenation. A victim's lawyer can assemble an evidence matrix that would include anecdotal evidence as well as the scientific evidence already referenced in this book. An expert medical assessment would be needed to examine the circumstances of each case to determine if there was a loss to the victim as a result of the disclosure failure. The scales of justice only require the evidence to tip the balance in favour of there being a loss due to the failure.

In the real world of clinical practice, some doctors are telling their patients about hyperbaric oxygenation, nevertheless other patients are not being told.[81] Also, in the circumstances of Dr A's patient described here, public and private healthcare in many parts of the globe including Ireland would pay for hyperbaric oxygenation to help avoid the amputation, yet Cochrane Reviews' authors don't tell one this or explain the scientific reasons for this.

The differences in the disclosure of information by medical professionals between countries could be partly explained by the editorial policy of Cochrane Reviews.

When the authors of the Cochrane Reviews in hyperbaric oxygenation decided to do this above review, they narrowed the focus to randomised trials and stated that: 'We aimed to include all randomised controlled trials comparing the clinical effects of HBOT with no HBOT (no treatment or sham) for healing of bone fractures and fracture non-unions.' However, the authors also reported that, 'no trials met the inclusion criteria.'

There is a need to be direct and honest without offending anyone. It will be seen in this chapter on the law of disclosure that these two quotations alone from the authors of the Cochrane Reviews in a legal scenario could be used as corroborative

---

[81] Melamed, Y., 'Hyperbaric Oxygen Therapy (Hbo) for Radiation Necrosis-Physician Awareness is Required', *Harefuah*, Vol. 157, No. 8, (2018) pp. 517-19

evidence against the interest of the authors in their own clinical practice. In a legal scenario, corroborative evidence is used to support the evidence of a witness. The point already made in this book is that they should not have looked for or expected randomised trials due to the Nuremberg Code (meaning to include Helsinki Declaration and European Convention etc.). Also, the law on disclosure should have been explained by the authors to account for the fact that no trials met the inclusion data.

It is however important to note a major problem for Cochrane Reviews' editorial policy for authors and their readers. The authors fail to explain that the absence of randomised controlled trials is likely because, in the current scenario, the Nuremberg Code prohibits randomising humans for controlled trials because of the known benefits.

In the absence of trials that met the authors' inclusion criteria, the authors go on to make several problematic legal errors. Cochrane Reviews, in the above case, used the words: 'Good quality clinical trials are needed to define the role, if any, of HBOT in the treatment of these injuries.' There is a possibility of bias in a legal sense on the part of the authors, and the choice of the words 'if any' must be considered with caution.

Nonetheless, the use of the phrase 'if any', meaning 'if any benefit', is as dangerous as suggesting that there are no known benefits for fracture healing on the best available evidence at the time. The use of this phrase also gives the wrong impression that one's limb is not at an increased risk of amputation if one does not use hyperbaric oxygenation.

Think of the dangerous legal and reputational problems brought upon the orthopaedic surgeon Dr A if the fracture non-union led to the complications above and one tried to defend the failure by saying: 'I did not tell the patient because Cochrane Reviews stated under the implications for practice summary:

'There is insufficient evidence to support or refute the use of hyperbaric oxygen therapy for the treatment of fractures, whether to aid healing of acute injuries or as a therapy for established non-union. Further evidence should be generated from trials that are ongoing at the time of writing.'

The report also states: 'This review failed to locate any randomised trial evidence to support or refute the treatment of fractures with hyperbaric oxygen therapy.' It further states: 'This systematic review failed to locate any relevant clinical evidence to support or refute the effectiveness of HBOT.'

There is a stalemate situation. In other parts of the globe, the Nuremberg Code is adhered to and randomising is unlawful, and Cochrane Reviews will not approve for general practice now or in the future because there are no randomised controlled trials overcoming the inclusion criteria. It's 10 years since the review in this example and it has not been withdrawn.

If all this evidence was being explained to a judge or jury, a victim's lawyer could put it simply. The legal problem with Cochrane Reviews is that it's not adequately reporting on the best clinical evidence available at the time and/or using modern scientific analysis tools to show how it's working because of the editorial exclusion criteria as it relates to hyperbaric oxygenation. It's like putting one's back up against the wall and one knows the wall is there, nonetheless one must report that one cannot see the wall.

So unfortunately for this surgeon's conduct, Dr A, a victim's lawyer has powerful cross-examination artillery from the language of the authors. In cross-examination of a defence witness the victim's lawyer could use a case report that did not reach Cochrane Reviews' inclusion criteria. Sorry to say for a witness in this scenario, even the review gives references to case reports that give reasons for the role of hyperbaric oxygenation in bone healing that the patient might consider significant. A victim's lawyer in Europe could show that hyperbaric oxygenation can be paid for by private medical insurance and state insurance, however the Food and Drug Administration does not approve non-union fracture.

The use of the words here 'if any' in the review could be the tort of negligent misrepresentation as it could be understood to mean that there is no known scientific evidence of benefit for hyperbaric oxygenation or having a role for delayed healing of a fracture or a fracture non-union.

This book is primarily to help one understand about balanced disclosure. To remain relevant, the editors of Cochrane Reviews need to understand the legal duty of balanced disclosure on authors of clinical practice guidelines and medical professionals when making disclosure to patients. As explained in earlier chapters, what should be disclosed is from a reasonable person in the patient's position and all of this is governed by law.

For people who opted for hyperbaric oxygenation, the available scientific analysis of why it should help is likely to be considered significant by them.

The legal problem with Cochrane Reviews may be better understood by the evidence matrix available to victim's lawyers discussed in this book.

There are further legal problems by attempting to persuade others to conduct randomised trials on humans. The first legal problems for medical professionals, due to the Nuremberg Code, commence at the clinical trial recruitment stage. Let's say that patients are needed with a non-union open tibial fracture.

A doctor seeking to recruit someone where there is planned to be a placebo or controlled group must disclose to that person the scientific and case report evidence matrix available at the time. One must give all the information that the person would consider significant as explained in this book. This must include the scientific reasons why it would be increasing the risk of complications such as pain, infection and possible amputation not to take hyperbaric oxygenation.

Nevertheless, in a law case about the legality of a randomised trial (required to be in the inclusion criteria), a fact finder such as a judge or jury must place oneself in the position of the patient with the non-union open tibial fracture. One must consider the patient's values and the possible complications. Would that person with the non-union open tibial fracture, if given the evidence matrix, be unlikely to agree to be part of a process of randomisation, where one could end up in the controlled or placebo group with no hyperbaric oxygenation given and an increased likelihood of losing a limb?

The second legal problem of the balanced disclosure consideration is the unlawful and unethical issue of asking people to take part in such a clinical trial and increasing the risk for them of complications and possible amputation. The legal references, in the COVID-19 chapter on depriving one of known benefits, verify this.

Nevertheless, the so-called 'poor quality data' is evidence of clinical findings of improvements that can be supported by an evidence matrix, with ample evidence to prohibit randomising humans. The data may have information about reported rapid recovery, the improvement in the quality of fracture union, the scientific reasons as to why reduced inflammation occurs and reduced pain and time in pain occurs.

The further conundrum here is that in Japan and other parts of the globe, medical professionals often decide against a randomised controlled trial due to the ethical reason that it's unnecessary. Imagine improvements being reported in Japan or even in the *British Medical Journal* on a non-randomised trial without a controlled or placebo group, and the authors of Cochrane Reviews saying the evidence is of poor quality. The expression 'poor quality' may simply mean it's not a randomised controlled trial or it's a single case report (n=1) or the numbers in the trial were small. Nevertheless, Cochrane Reviews' inclusion criteria is not met. Nonetheless, the authors ill-advisedly fail, from both the authors and the patient's view, to explain that these experienced medical professionals considered that a randomised trial was not possible for ethical and legal reasons because the ill patients in a controlled group could not be put to the risk of being deprived of the known benefits.

In considering hyperbaric oxygenation, one needs to reconsider the controversy about the perceived need for randomised controlled trials in the first place. One has seen in this book that modern technology can prove the benefit of oxygenation and hyperbaric oxygenation to injured tissue at a cellular level. This is just a modern way of illustrating evidence-based medicine.

Unfortunately, with hyperbaric oxygenation, the well-intentioned authors may see the need for randomised trials exclusively to persuade sceptics within the medical community or simply for drug approval agencies, so it becomes part of the reimbursement list from insurance companies. There is also a fear of 'tarnishing the credibility of hyperbaric medicine' within the medical community.[82]

---

[82] Chandrasekhar Krishnamurti, 'Historical Aspects of Hyperbaric Physiology and Medicine', *Diving and Hyperbaric Medicine*, (2019). Available online at:

Having learned from the COVID-19 pandemic that decisions about advising patients on treatment options were contrary to disclosure and consent medical law, one needs to consider if calls for randomising humans are actually a barrier to advancements in healthcare caused by the editorial policy of Cochrane Reviews. Reasonable people understand the necessity for blinded randomised controlled trials with a controlled or placebo group for a pharmaceutical drug prior to approval.

However, oxygenation and hyperbaric oxygenation already have an established place in science, as a general and approved practice and healing agent for diseases or tissue injury. One cannot emphasise it enough that, in a legal scenario, it's easy to prove that without oxygen our cells die. The editors of Cochrane Reviews need to stay relevant to the urgent need for doctors to practice within the law of disclosure and informed consent. It would have helped in this example report about fracture healing and treating fracture non-union if reference was made to the universal gas laws, the scientific explanation for the delivery of oxygenation and hyperbaric oxygenation to plasma and injured tissue. The evidence matrix in a legal scenario has already been discussed. To further the evidence-based practice objective of Cochrane Reviews to help professionals advise patients in a balanced way, to comply with the law, one must radically change the editorial policy in the section of the review called 'Plain Language Summary', as regards the use of hyperbaric oxygenation. The years of medical evidence have inspired the legal jurisprudence and the editors who, after taking their own legal advice, are well equipped to set out and create an evidence

---

https://www.researchgate.net/publication/332771676_Historical_Aspects_of_Hyperbaric_Physiology_and_Medicine

matrix for hyperbaric oxygenation, such as the gas laws information in addition to the scientific use of blood analysis markers for inflammation, inducing stem cell production, increased angiogenesis, and infection markers.

**Conflicts of Cochrane Reviews' Authors**

There is an example of the legal and ethical problems for the editors of Cochrane Reviews in a comment about the manuscript of this book that I received from a well-meaning Dr X in an email. This Dr X is an author for Cochrane Reviews. Dr X's email stated: 'What is not acceptable ethically to me is the widespread adoption of HBO as a routine measure in the absence of better evidence.'

Is this email a reflection of the politics in medicine to gain or maintain credibility with the Food and Drug Administration or other medical professionals? Medical professionals who advocate for hyperbaric oxygenation and are trying to advance the cause may be taking an over-cautious stance regarding evidence. A well-intended purist position may nonetheless be depriving patients of balanced disclosure and putting them at risk of adverse events.

Dr X's comment may help to answer the question: Why do leading countries around the globe differ in healthcare treatments offered? Why are Japan, China and other parts of Europe using hyperbaric oxygenation as a routine measure for indications that Cochrane Reviews' authors are inspiring others to conduct randomised controlled trials? The problem is that in one part of the globe there is compliance with the Nuremberg Code and the law of balanced disclosure, and in another part of the globe there is not equal compliance.

Is this email an example of Dr X being unethical, by implying that medical professionals are not acting ethically by suggesting a patient use hyperbaric oxygenation or even try it? Is Dr X dissuading the other doctor from giving balanced information? In legal terms, it's similar to one doctor accusing another of quackery, which may be dissuading the doctor from giving balanced information. However, Dr X's position overlooks the legal requirement that the decision-maker must be the patient.

What one may understand is that Dr X's statement that it's 'not acceptable ethically' to offer hyperbaric oxygenation as a 'routine measure' is based on his own view of what is acceptable and unacceptable evidence to tell a patient. Is this what Dr X thinks should be said to a patient? Is the innuendo that Dr X's ethical code is not based on the patient's values? However, in this case, if one's understanding of Dr X's position is not to make disclosure until there is 'better evidence', then Dr X's reasoning is the direct opposite to Dr X's legal obligation to explain in a balanced way the best (scientific) evidence available at the time to enable the patient to decide.

Nonetheless, this conservatism or mistaken ethics is part of the legal problem and part of the editorial problem of Cochrane Reviews. However, based on the law of informed consent, in Japan, hyperbaric oxygenation for a new indication can become a routine measure if the treatment becomes the patient's preferred option. Dr X's concept of its application being unethical until there is 'better evidence' does not apply.

If, however, one is a medical professional and one agrees with this email from Dr X just quoted, then one is in danger of giving artillery to the victim's lawyer.

It's legally problematic if the doctor used Dr X's reasoning to not disclose the known scientific benefits and clinical evidence to an ill patient in the position of Dr A's patient with the non-union open tibial fracture.

Also, there may be other Cochrane Reviews authors who are conflicted or biased in a legal sense, because authors of the review may themselves in clinical practice have treated a patient in circumstances where there was an invalid informed consent. This could be because some of the significant benefits of hyperbaric oxygenation for a medical condition were not disclosed. They may be conflicted for failing to comply with the legal duty of candour to point out to a patient that another doctor failed to make disclosure and they were treated with an invalid informed consent.

A surgeon or an anaesthetist, as authors of a Cochrane review, would be conflicted or biased in a legal sense if they were involved in a similar amputation, following complications of Dr A's patient with a non-union fracture without disclosure about hyperbaric oxygenation.

As seen earlier in this book, clinical trials do not take place in many countries because the Nuremberg Code is followed, and randomised trials are considered unnecessary and unethical. This is because of the known benefits. In Japan for example, using hyperbaric oxygenation for neurological dysfunction is a general and approved practice. However, authors of Cochrane Reviews may be conflicted if in clinical practice one did not make disclosure to one's patient who had brain injury of the known benefits. Again, depriving someone of information or balanced disclosure on those universally accepted and known benefits, as referred to in this book, amounts to assault and battery if there is an invalid informed consent. Unfortunately for those editors dealing with hyperbaric oxygenation, they are aware of the known benefits that should be disclosed.

Regrettably, the problem for the lawyer defending the medical professionals' conduct is that it's not commonly known what the legal requirements are with regard to a valid informed consent.

Remember the doctors in the French city of Opelousas hospital, in Louisiana, or the doctors in Wuhan, China, who were administering hyperbaric oxygenation to the first COVID-19 case (n=1)? Is the thinking of Dr X, one of the authors of Cochrane Reviews, that these doctors were unethical to suggest hyperbaric oxygenation as a routine measure? If this is the case, then Dr X is legally wrong.

What's problematic and easy to correct are the sections of Cochrane Reviews like the 'Author's Conclusions' or the 'Plain Language Summary'. What is easy to correct is the language that is likely to be ethically and legally problematic regarding the law of disclosure and informed consent. The busy medical professional would be helped by the editorial policy keeping abreast of the radical changes in the law of informed consent.

There is too much emphasis placed on extracted empirical data or inferences based on the absence of data and failing to explain the absence. The authors should explain that the absence of data may be because of the Nuremberg Code, European Convention or the Helsinki Declaration. This may explain why Japan, China, Europe and other parts of the globe are ahead of the US. The information and language used by Cochrane Reviews is likely to be repeated in the doctor's clinical practice guidelines or directly by a doctor to a patient. This is a medico-legal problem, as there is insufficient information on the risks to adverse outcomes in not using other treatment options.

It's valuable to consider another medical condition and consider how, by way of example, a clinical practice's guidelines may not help the medical professionals practice within the law of disclosure and informed consent.

## An Example of the Clinical Practice Guidelines' Problems

The *Journal of Crohn's and Colitis* is used in this chapter to show by way of example as one sees it the need for a change in the editorial format for guidelines.[83] The journal published the third European Evidence-Based Consensus on the Diagnosis and Management of Crohn's disease in 2016. The questions relevant to the law of balanced disclosure and informed consent in this example are:

1. Are immune suppressants and pain medications prescribed for Inflammatory Bowel Diseases unnecessary and redundant?
2. Is most of rectum removal surgery for Inflammatory Bowel Diseases unnecessary and redundant?
3. Is there another way of treating hypoxic Inflammatory Bowel Diseases that would be the patient's treatment of choice?
4. Is the European Consensus wrong or misleading because it says that 'Crohn's disease is a lifelong disease?'

---

[83] Paolo Gionchetti et al., '3rd European Evidence-based Consensus on the Diagnosis and Management of Crohn's Disease 2016: Part 2: Surgical Management and Special Situations', *Journal of Crohn's and Colitis*, Vol. 11, No. 2, (2017), pp. 135–49. Available online at: https://academic.oup.com/ecco-jcc/article/11/2/135/2456548#supplementary-data

If the reasonable person in the patient's position considers what is said in this chapter to be significant, this reasonable person may say that treatments currently 'recommended' in this third European Consensus will be superseded and made redundant by hyperbaric oxygenation if the law of disclosure and informed consent is properly complied with.

One may ask why one has chosen Inflammatory Bowel Disease as an example for discussion of where clinical practice guidelines have been legally problematic. An issue is that it's worth analysing because the Food and Drug Administration have not approved this condition, however hyperbaric oxygenation is an approved and routine measure in other parts of the globe. Furthermore, this analysis is chosen because there is a large number of people suffering from this condition and a lot of benefit will come to them if what is said in this chapter is accepted and becomes approved in general practice. The risk taken in not using hyperbaric oxygenation in Inflammatory Bowel Disease is a grave adverse outcome for someone who was misinformed that the only treatment option left was to have surgery and have one's rectum removed.

Nevertheless, if a clinical case report shows that an impressive 18 people out of 40 had complete remission and a further 17 patients of the same 40 had partial remission and 100% has some benefit then the courts could possibly not only find there was no consent but dramatically and unusually overturn the opinion of the medical community not to have hyperbaric oxygenation as part of standard care.[84] The *Journal of Crohn's and*

---

[84] Dulai, P.S., Gleeson, M.W., Taylor, D., Holubar, S.D., Buckey, J.C. and Siegel, C.A., 'Systematic review: The safety and efficacy of hyperbaric oxygen therapy for inflammatory bowel disease', *Alimentary Pharmacology & Therapeutics*, (2014), pp. 1266-1275

*Colitis* said in October 2021 within the section Current Practice Position 4.5 that: 'Hyperbaric oxygen therapy may achieve clinical response in UC.'

There are two significant and distinct risks involved here arising from the editorial format. The medical or legal professionals being complacent about potential litigation is risky and dangerous. The patient is exposed to the risk of an adverse event resulting in a lifelong disease or life-changing adverse surgery. Another reason for using this example is that Long COVID Syndrome has caused similar hypoxic tissue injury and hyperbaric oxygenation has reversed this tissue injury along with many other symptoms.

Even the risk of medical professionals failing to disclose the treatment is likely to have serious consequences for them if a claim is made, because it's so serious for the patient. I also chose Inflammatory Bowel Disease as I have first-hand anecdotal experience in Galway and Dublin from people who were told to have surgery and avoided it.

The authors' work preparing the consensus is commendable, but if the format in the document is a pathway to legal problems and inherently dangerous, then this format to avoid litigation needs to change. For that reason, there are many reported cases of complete remission or part remission from Inflammatory Bowel Disease where hyperbaric oxygenation or nutrition changes were used, however, because patients are not informed about these options, there is a significant legal and ethical problem. Because the drug treatment for Inflammatory Bowel Disease has been so debilitating, nevertheless, without a cure and the surgery that has such adverse consequences, this anomaly will soon come to an end.

Seven thousand gastroenterologists in Europe need to see that they have medico-legal problems on the horizon. They unfortunately prescribe medications or surgical interventions unlawfully because there is in place an invalid informed consent. This is by reason of the fact that their patients have not been given balanced disclosure about the hyperbaric oxygenation options, or the need to use the special skillset of a nutrition professional who is trained to take the patient through an in-depth educational experience. For example, a period of prolonged fasting is an alternative to some temporary gastrointestinal surgery to enable healing. In other words, would one like to be told that one can fast such as doing cycles from one to 40 days with no food at all except one's abdominal fat? One just drinks water under a professional's supervision to allow natural healing, rather than taking the risk of two invasive gastrointestinal surgeries that give one a temporary stoma bag. This fasting as referenced in the Holy Bible is common for many medical issues using experienced nutrition professionals, where the body's hybrid system goes into ketosis and burns fat and makes things called ketones, which fuel the body.

From the view of a victim's lawyer, this third European Consensus is artillery for victims. Due to the potential litigation and the obligation to make disclosure on the treatment options for Inflammatory Bowel Disease, a layperson's view will be the deciding factor.

The Consensus says that Crohn's disease is a lifelong disease. However, if one studies the case reports referenced in this chapter on hyperbaric oxygenation, one will see cases of full remission and that, in one study, all patients under review (100%) showed 'a remarkably favourable clinical improvement'.[85]

A victim's lawyer will show that there was frequent total remission and will also use the evidence matrix using science as explained earlier. However, because the drugs recommended are said to only aim to manage rather than cure the disease, this is corroborating evidence to prove that, in comparison to hyperbaric oxygenation, typical drug treatments are inadequate. The standard drugs recommended are known as tumour necrosis factor (TNF) inhibitors such as Humira.

This example is not confined to Crohn's disease and one must always think in terms of what the drug is prescribed to do and compare this to the science of why and what hyperbaric oxygenation is known to do. This is partly to heal injured tissue and reduce inflammation.[86]

With Inflammatory Bowel Disease, a reduction in blood flow known as ischaemia results in arterial insufficiency, which results in inflammation, hypoxic tissue injury at cellular level, bleeding ulcers and frequent infections which are invariably present. One has already seen how technology can detect shortage of oxygen, inflammation and infection markers, backed up by wireless inspection endoscopic video recordings. Professor James explains that 'tissues are collections of cells, each surrounded by watery interstitial fluid, and the watery content can increase because the damaged walls of blood vessels leak'.

---

[85] Ibid.

[86] Zhang Y., Lv Y., Liu Y.J., Yang C., Hu H.J., Meng X.E., et al., 'Hyperbaric Oxygen Therapy in Rats Attenuates Ischemia-reperfusion Testicular Injury Through Blockade of Oxidative Stress, Suppression of Inflammation, and Reduction of Nitric Oxide Formation', *Urology*, Vol. 82, No. 2, (2013), pp. 9-489

The first powerful impeachment evidence to unseat any defence evidence is that the biological phenomena of hypoxic tissue injury at cellular level in Inflammatory Bowel Disease is biologically similar to radiation-induced hypoxic tissue injury at cellular level during cancer treatments. If hyperbaric oxygenation is used for one, it defies logic not to use it for the other. In a legal scenario, this is scientifically corroborated evidence that strengthens or confirms already existing scientific evidence of its use for radiation tissue injury. The evidence is there that it also accords with general and approved practice.

Regrettably for doctors, their defence lawyers have an uphill battle caused by the inconsistencies and contradictions that a victim's lawyer can use in cross-examination. In the real world of science, in the same or other hospitals, hyperbaric oxygenation is the standard of care for tissue injury, inflammation and infection. The disparity of care between Japan and the US is that it's a routine measure in Japan for Inflammatory Bowel Disease, whereas the Food and Drug Administration has not given approval despite the inconsistencies in refusing.

However, in a legal scenario, what is problematic is that it's easy to prove that hyperbaric oxygenation is used as standard of care if the tissue injury is caused by, for example, radiation treatment for cancer patients. Put another way, as in the *Dunne v The National Maternity Hospital* case already mentioned, the court took a view that the 'general and approved practice' has defects that would be apparent to anyone giving the matter reasonable consideration.[87]

It's time for the medical community to pause here, as it would help to consider the artillery given to the victim's lawyers by a

---

[87] Ibid., Dunne (an infant) v The National Maternity Hospital (1989)

sentence in the Consensus, which explains that nothing more can be done except surgery. The document says: 'The care of CD is now primarily in the hands of medical gastroenterologists. However, many patients will require multiple surgeries during their disease.' The consensus also states: 'Unfortunately, surgery is not curative as the disease inexorably recurs in many patients.' Regarding the known successes with hyperbaric oxygenation as stated in this chapter, people are not warned of the risks if they don't have the treatments. Nonetheless, people are informed that they need to surgically remove their rectum and attach a stoma bag or are meant to have other life-changing unnecessary surgery.

Further ammunition for the victim's lawyer is that, later in this book, other treatments are mentioned in part two of the third European Consensus, but unfortunately not in a way that is helpful to the medical professional regarding the law of informed consent. Within that paragraph, it mentions 'hyperbaric oxygen' and a footnote about hyperbaric oxygen. Nutrition and other alternative treatments are briefly mentioned; however the Consensus says these additional treatments are 'not recommended for standard practice'.

The Consensus does not help clinicians because it fails to give a balanced explanation of how hyperbaric oxygenation or nutrition might help and has given remission to others. One might counter argue on behalf of the authors of the Consensus that the Consensus is not designed to deal with what is suggested here. Whatever the view, to avoid litigation doctors need better and more balanced guidelines, to provide professional help that will keep them within the law.

To provide some context of the disparity in giving information on treatment options, the Consensus' authors should consider that 14 medical indications have Food and Drug Administration approval for using hyperbaric oxygenation compared to nine medical indications for Humira.

In this discussion, the helpful question that must be answered in a legal scenario is: What would a judge determine if they put themselves in the shoes of the reasonable person in the patient's position? The judges must imagine themselves in a position where gastroenterologists had the chronically ill patient on years of TNF immune suppression medication (Anti-TNF therapy) as recommended by the Consensus, without the person being told about hyperbaric oxygenation as a treatment option.

In the trial, the victim will be able to give evidence on scientific proof referenced in this book and all the circumstantial and corroborative evidence available as proof in a legal scenario of success for one patient (n=1) and/or in this case the reported cases on hyperbaric oxygenation and/or nutrition options. What would a judge or jury determine the reasonable person in the patient's position would determine if a surgeon recommended removing the patient's rectum and using a stoma bag or some other surgery in the gastrointestinal tract without informing the person about all patients (100%) who showed remarkable clinical improvement and the supporting scientific proof or the pre- and post-biopsies? Unfortunately, for the lawyers defending the medical community, the judge's answer is not a medical view, which is the key to understanding the amount of invalid informed consents.

An example of further problems for lawyers for the medical community in attempting to defend this scenario before a judge or jury is that abundant impeachment or unseating evidence is easily found in the same journal. The victim's lawyer can show that, if the doctor took reasonable care, the information in the

*Journal of Crohn's and Colitis* could be found on the same website as the third European Consensus. There are articles published in the media and medical journals on the use of hyperbaric oxygenation for Inflammatory Bowel Diseases. One medical report is based on 17 studies involving 613 patients (286 Crohn's disease and 327 ulcerative colitis) over a number of years.[88] The overall response rate was 86%. Again, the victim's lawyer will point to the anomaly. They can show that other doctors differ in opinion from the consensus because hyperbaric oxygenation is used by patients. They can show that the treatment has been successful.

A reported use of hyperbaric oxygenation for the conditions discussed in the Consensus was in a letter to the editor of the *British Medical Journal* in 1977.[89] This letter was written at a time when the law in the UK was wrongly interpreted by its Supreme Court (then the House of Lords) when the doctor 'knew best' scenario was applied and the patient was incorrectly deprived of one's legal right to be given balanced disclosure.

Further powerful impeachment evidence that a victim's lawyer can use to unseat a defence expert witness is in the *Textbook of Hyperbaric Medicine* (2017) by the neurosurgeon Kewal K Jain and other authors. The extent to which the European gastroenterologists can be unseated by failing to take

---

[88] The report says: 'Given the subjectivity in physician-reported response to therapy, sensitivity analyses were performed including only studies reporting endoscopic follow-up of disease activity. The overall response rate was 86% (85% CD, 88% UC). The overall response rate for said perineal CD was 88% (18/40 complete healing, 17/40 partial healing). Of the 40 UC patients with endoscopic follow-up reported, the overall response rate to HBOT was 100%.'

Ibid., Dulai, P.S. et al. (2014)

[89] The letter referenced a study by Watanuki T. et al., 'A study on the effects of hyperbaric oxygenation on intestinal paralysis', (1970) [Br Med J. 1977 Jun 18; 1(6076): 1602.PMCID: PMC1607375]. Available online at: https://www.ncbi.nlm.nih.gov/pmc/articles/PMC1607375/?page=1

reasonable care to make disclosure is that the textbook has an entire chapter devoted to Hyperbaric Oxygenation and Gastroenterology.

A successful case study from Egypt is discussed. A case report references recovery using hyperbaric oxygenation in 1994, reported in the 2016 edition of the *British Medical Journal* in the chapter Open Gastroenterology.[90] As this chapter is a tool to avoid being sued, it's valuable nonetheless to be aware that the report says: 'After 40 sessions, the patient's general condition improved remarkably along with complete remission of her colonic symptoms. Therefore, surgery was deferred. After that, we systematically offered HBO sessions to patients with refractory UC.'

If what is said here is accurate and one believes it to be so, and the reasonable person decides to use hyperbaric oxygenation, how quickly will the many thousands of gastroenterologists become redundant? This means that if the patient decides to use hyperbaric oxygenation, the current standard of care treatments in gastroenterology for inflammatory diseases will be redundant and superseded by hyperbaric oxygenation.

In a further study, the results showed that hyperbaric oxygen therapy did 'not improve the effects of standardized treatment in a severe attack of ulcerative colitis'.[91] However, this clinical case

---

[90] Bekheit, M., Baddour, N., Katri, K., Taher, Y., El Tobgy, K. and Mousa, E., 'Hyperbaric oxygen therapy stimulates colonic stem cells and induces mucosal healing in patients with refractory ulcerative colitis: a prospective case series', *BMJ Open Gastroenterology*, Vol. 3, No. 1, (2016), p.e000082

[91] Pagoldh, M., Hultgren, E., Arnell, P. and Eriksson, A., 'Hyperbaric oxygen therapy does not improve the effects of standardized treatment in a severe attack of ulcerative colitis: a prospective randomized study', Scandinavian Journal of Gastroenterology, Vol. 48, No. 9, (2013) pp. 1033-40

report could be used by a victim's lawyer as a case of 'too little treatment too late' or 'justice delayed is justice denied'.

### Oxygen Levels Affect Cellular Metabolism

The Nobel Prize in Medicine 2019 was won by three scientists who, according to the Nobel Prize committee, 'established the basis for our understanding of how oxygen affects cellular metabolism and physiological function. Their discoveries have also paved the way for promising new strategies to fight anaemia, cancer and many other diseases'. Oxygenation is constantly healing the injured or leaking tissue at cellular level for the wear and tear of daily living.

The world community is on the move and changing. Worldwide, private investment bankers are adopting their investments to 'green' investments because their customers want this. The same is happening in medicine and this includes nutrition.

### Nutrition and Fasting

This is an example of the dangers of ignoring science until there are randomised controlled trials. In 2016, the Nobel Prize in Medicine was won by Professor Yoshinori Ohsumi of Tokyo University because his team proved how fasting activates autophagy. Laboratory experiments showed that this helps slow down the ageing process and positively impacts cell renewal. It would cause harm to tell someone that there is 'no evidence' that fasting in the manner described is good for one's health. There is no need for randomised controlled trials on humans to show that fasting is beneficial for one's health. It is becoming increasingly accepted that encouraging the use of nutrition professionals is the correct pathway despite the claims of arbitrary controlled trials on humans for nutrition. Dr Jason Fung (a Canadian-based nephrologist) and Jimmy Moore's research on fasting have improved people's quality of life. Their book *The Complete Guide to Fasting: Heal Your Body Through Intermittent, Alternate-Day, and Extended Fasting* combined with Professor Ohsumi's discovery could be used as impeachment or unseating evidence. Their information could be used against the interest of the doctor who fails to discuss food as a medicine along with the value of nutrition, diet, lifestyle and fasting before medical intervention.

**Functional Medicine**

In obtaining valid informed consent, remember that treatment options have roots in different movements of medical thinking. An example to be aware of is that a rapidly growing movement of like-minded clinicians comprises doctors, nutrition professionals, psychologists and pharmacists who are called Functional Medicine. This is often explained as 'root cause medicine', where clinicians and nutrition professionals practice with a different emphasis, especially when dealing with chronic disease. If needed, motivational psychologists can help people stay on track with lifestyle, food, fasting and nutrition advice.

One of the best-known international advocates for this movement is Dr Mark Hyman, based at the Cleveland Clinic in the US, who says: 'Food isn't like medicine, it is medicine, and it's our number one tool for creating vibrant health we deserve.' This movement also has its vocal critics, but in all of this debate the critics must remember the relevant law: Each client has a legal right to decide on the treatment options and obtain balanced information prior to giving a valid informed consent to any medical intervention. Functional medicine puts the client in the major decision-making position, but even these professionals would help bring about the culture needed in society to advocate for the legal right to be centre-stage in decision making. Large International Functional Medicine conferences have taken place in the US, the UK and Ireland.

The majority of the current medical community are well placed for changes in the demands of the public to avoid medication and a growing preference for a new type of guidance in healthcare. Medical schools have trained doctors in the art of diagnosis. Doctors are open to change. Their calling is for their patients.[92] [93] People diagnosed with a life-threatening or severe life-altering disease want to know all the healthcare options in detail.

Nutrition professionals are especially skilled in food, nutrition, fasting and diet. Nevertheless, what could be legally problematic is that if doctors proceed with a treatment option, such as long-term immunosuppressants, without advising their patients to first see a nutrition professional. It may happen in a future legal scenario that it will not be enough to simply say: One encouraged the patient to eat healthy, participate in exercise and avoid smoking. A referral to experts in this area may be the safer option before a lifetime of treating someone with Pharma.

For the wrong reasons, clinicians may feel constrained in their approach and not want to step outside the box of the accepted norms. There are no black or white solutions, and everyone suffers as a result of this. One hopes this chapter will help promote an objective discussion and debate about the options

---

[92] The Institute for Functional Medicine (website: https://www.ifm.org/about/)

[93] https://www.schoolandcollegelistings.com/XX/Unknown/555511547963933/Functional-Medicine-Conference-Ireland

available to different healthcare professionals, groups and patients.

**Change is with us**

Home use hyperbaric cabins will become popular even though they may provide less pressure and less percentage oxygen concentration than the ones used in some hospitals or private commercial chambers. Care must be taken not to discourage people from using oxygenation at normal atmospheric pressure or increased pressure and increased levels of oxygenation because of the known benefits described in this book.

Nevertheless, medical professionals making false or misleading statements or making disparaging remarks against hyperbaric chambers used in the home (with less than 1.4 ATA) may amount to the legal tort of false misrepresentation. A definition of hyperbaric oxygenation that implies a treatment under 1.4 ATA is outside the definition of hyperbaric oxygenation is misleading and wrong. Also, using a smaller percentage of oxygen than 100% at greater than atmospheric is nonetheless hyperbaric oxygenation therapy.

One is not seeking to be alarmist or overstating trends in litigation. This chapter is a discussion about the individual medical professional avoiding being the one to be sued.

# Chapter Five:

# Duty of Candour, Disclosure and Informed Consent to Medical Intervention

The problem of failing in the duty of candour and disclosure about adverse events resulting in loss endures indefinitely until it is disclosed and resolved. To avoid dangerous pitfalls, one should obtain one's own independent legal advice as a medical professional. One may be shocked when one discovers that, not only is there an obligation to fulfil one's duty of candour to the injured party for an adverse event, but failing to do so will have ongoing professional indemnity insurance cover complications. It's not worth the risk and is more beneficial the sooner one makes disclosure, and especially while one is insured and in practice.

The Health Service Executive in Ireland and elsewhere know that it's necessary to deal with a duty of candour to make disclosure to patients about adverse events openly and honestly. In the next chapter, one will see that there are applications for hyperbaric oxygenation that are recommended as standard care and even covered by medical insurance; nevertheless, patients were put at risk of loss and harm, as they were not told. If patients were put at risk due to a failure to inform patients about hyperbaric oxygenation for other medical conditions that would have been beneficial, the same duty of candour and exposure to being sued successfully applies. For all of these situations, people were put at risk of having an adverse medical event because they were not told. The question is, how long after the adverse event can one be sued successfully? There is no end period for fulfilling the duty of candour.

### Statute of Limitations

One may ask, what if the adverse event such as bowel removal surgery or the amputation of a non-union fractured leg occurred years ago? This is a Statute of Limitations issue, and the laws in each country differ. In the case of the UK, the new interpretation of the law on disclosure and informed consent came about in March 2015 and the decision makes it retrospective in its application. The Statute of Limitations law is very similar in both Ireland, the UK and elsewhere.

A statute of the limitation period does not necessarily commence to run at the time of the injury. In 2019, the Irish Supreme Court, in considering a delay in issuing proceedings for a man who had contracted MRSA, said: 'This timespan runs either from the occurrence of the wrong, which is the ordinary rule, or exceptionally from the date of knowledge, meaning when the plaintiff "first had knowledge" of the identity of the defendant and of the fact of significant injury and that the wrong was attributable in whole or in part to the act or omission which is alleged to constitute negligence.'[94]

---

[94] Oliver O'Sullivan v Ireland and others (May 2019)

Even if one was not told about the options, there might not have been significant injury or any loss due to the particular circumstances of the trajectory of the disease or the treatment given, which must be investigated by medical experts.

**Cervical Cancer Screening**

Learning by one's mistakes is to be avoided. In Ireland, the whole community unfortunately learned by mistakes made with grave consequences. In the law case of *Ruth Morrissey v Ireland*, the Irish Supreme Court affirmed the right to be told about adverse events. This right was conceded in court by the Irish Health Service Executive.[95] In Ireland, some 220 women were wrongly diagnosed as being negative for cervical cancer screening; when the error was discovered that they, in fact ,had cancer, this information was initially not disclosed to them.

As a hospital manager or as a medical professional one must take special care as this law governing the 'duty of candour' has far reaching and surprising legal and ethical consequences. While the patient's right to candour is embodied in law in different ways in different jurisdictions, there is an overlap with the law on the duty of disclosure (right to know) of treatment and diagnostic options and the right of patients to be informed that treatment or diagnostic opportunities were not disclosed and that adverse events occurred. The rights of patients include a right to be told about adverse events in civil law, however withholding information for an improper purpose under criminal law such as the prevention of corruption laws in Europe is not covered by this book.

[95] Morrissey & Anor v Health Service Executive & Ors [March 2020] IESC Available online at: https://www.bailii.org/ie/cases/IESC/2020/2020IESC6_0.html

Unfortunately for those lawyers defending civil cases for medical professionals dealing with the law of disclosure (right to know) prior to obtaining a valid informed consent, there is an overriding duty on medical professionals and hospital management to inform patients about adverse events no matter when the event occurred.

A law passed in the UK in 2008 made it obligatory to disclose adverse medical events as soon as possible after they occur.[96] In fact, it was not until September 2021 that the first prosecution in the UK took place, after which a hospital was fined for their failure to disclose a mistake during surgery.[97] In the US, similar laws apply.

### Candour About New Treatment or Diagnostic Options Elsewhere

What can be an exasperating situation for progressive doctors seeking updated equipment from hospital management can also be seriously problematic, regarding disclosure and informed consent law. There is an upside to this legally and ethically problematic scenario. A medical professional can use the law of regarding the duty of candour and the law of balanced disclosure and what would be an invalid informed consent as leverage to advance the argument for better services. A medical economist and a lawyer can also help here.

A medical professional, for example, may be agitating for hospital management to replace redundant or outdated radiation oncology diagnostic and treating equipment for treating cancer patients because there is safer and better equipment elsewhere.

---

[96] Health and Social Care Act (2008)

[97] University Hospitals Plymouth NHS Trust admitted the offence and paid a fine. It failed to disclose details relating to a surgical procedure.

The salesperson for equipment or the doctor may have explained to management that there has been a general improvement in outcomes in terms of quality of life or lives saved with the new equipment. In the meantime, without disclosure, an invalid informed consent is obtained and any medical intervention would be unlawful.

One may ask about a situation where the consultant or professional does not know about better equipment elsewhere. They must take reasonable care to keep themselves informed about new equipment. In any event, a hospital as a defendant is deemed to be aware of information in its records. One must take reasonable care to inform the patient where this new equipment is being used.

This situation is also potentially problematic as a general practitioner (GP) must also take reasonable care to advise and inform the patient where the best equipment and services are available. The duty of a GP is to take reasonable care to help the patient decide on treatment options and this includes selecting consultants or hospitals or other treatment options. Unfortunately, a judge may consider that a GP in an advisory role is not taking reasonable care if the GP does not inform a patient about treatment options.

Again, the information that must be disclosed by the GP is governed by law. A judge must determine if the GP took reasonable care to find out what the treatment options were. As explained, the EU Cross-Border Healthcare Directive widens the treatment options. Unfortunately, the GP in an advisory role on treatment options must take reasonable care to help the patient arrive at the best decision as regards a referral for the patient, as this is based on the patient's values and needs.

If one, as a GP, refers someone to any hospital or consultant without taking reasonable care to take an objective view about the consultant's equipment or outputs, then in this case, one would be wrong to think that there are no legal problems with this.

For balanced disclosure to a patient, a GP should consider the legal requirements on balanced disclosure and whether a judge would determine that a reasonable person in the patient's position might think that a GP should know.

**SPECT and PET Scans v Old MRI**

We have seen in this book the use of SPECT and PET scans for identifying areas of hypoxic tissue injury in the brain. We have seen in a legal scenario of (n=1) in which before and after SPECT scans can show neurological injury and recovery.

In circumstances where the hospitals only have or generally use inferior scanning equipment, such as older versions of MRI scans, the cause or fact of a neurological dysfunction may not be seen, and the patient may be incorrectly told that one does not have a neurological (tissue) injury. The patient's correct neurological diagnosis is missed; however the legal problem is that the patient should have been told about superior equipment elsewhere. This is a red flag warning of an example, as using the outdated MRI scan on a patient without good disclosure and a legitimate informed consent is an assault and battery in civil law in most countries.

If one searches the Internet about this outdated equipment issue, especially with the NHS in the UK, the journalists don't mention or seem to understand the importance of the law of disclosure and treatments with an invalid informed consent.

Nonetheless, this new equipment issue is a problematic legal scenario that people are learning about. Unfortunately for doctors it is universal, but this does not make it a legal defence. This scenario is in every branch of medicine and surgery in every part of the world and is seriously problematic in a legal and ethical way. The law is clear and gives rights to patients under domestic laws and international conventions. Telling the patient about the option to go elsewhere is the only answer. Notwithstanding anything said, this scenario is how disclosure and informed consent law brings back the power to the doctor, and allows them and the patient to work together.

**Problems about Published Research**

This is another issue when discussing prescription medicine. The issue is how trustworthy the evidence a medical professional relies on in everyday practice is and how balanced disclosure is made to patients about the problems with research.

Dr Marcia Angell, a physician and former editor of the prestigious *New England Journal of Medicine*, noted: 'It's no longer possible to trust most of the published research or rely on the authority of medical guidelines.'

Dr Aseem Malhotra, a London-based cardiologist, has the same kind of message as Dr Angell. Dr Malhotra is an adjunct professor of evidence-based medicine and a controversial, although highly respected bestselling author, and has highlighted the problems with the evidence. I was fortunate to be present when he delivered his guest talk at the 2017 Annual Functional

Medicine Conference, hosted by nutritionist Maev Creaven in Galway.[98] The talk can be viewed on YouTube.[99]

He pointed to a problem when he said that, of drugs approved by the Food and Drug Administration between 2000-2008, only 11% were actually genuinely innovative. Most were basically copies of old ones with minimal change to obtain approval and patent protection for a new product.[100]

This seems to be a continuing cycle; however I see the legal problems and say that the medical community and drug companies need independent legal counsel. What is a problem for drug companies in the civil and criminal courts is that it may be proved that the clinical trial was simply a tool for deception. In a time when stockbrokers make fortunes in shorting stock and the willingness of whistle-blowers to come forward, law cases are likely.

## Accountability of Professionals

If nurses and/or podiatrists working under a hospital consultant have administered daily dressings on a non-healing wound without making disclosure about hyperbaric oxygenation, and these professionals think that they are safe from being successfully sued, then, in this case, they are wrong. In fact, the patients have given an invalid informed consent. The treatment action is considered an assault in law. The recovery time will be quicker and the nurse or podiatrists must disclose information and lose business.

---

[98]https://www.schoolandcollegelistings.com/XX/Unknown/555511547963933/Functional-Medicine-Conference-Ireland

[99] Dr Aseem Malhotra, Keynote Presentation, (Nov 3rd, 2017). Available online at: https://www.youtube.com/watch?v=TbDS9m94uME&t=2s

[100] See footnote 99.

It's the same with a physiotherapist who is giving physiotherapy for, for example, a sports injury, a stroke or Parkinson's disease without disclosing information about hyperbaric oxygenation. Again, the physiotherapist must give balanced disclosure and potentially lose business because of the rapid improvement.

Nevertheless, with any rehabilitation for neurological dysfunction, whether one is a speech therapist or a physiotherapist, one must take reasonable care to explore the reasonable treatment options.

**Unnecessary Hysterectomies as an Example of Benefits of Disclosure?**

While rare, the stories of multiple unnecessary hysterectomies due to individual surgeons' oddities or idiosyncrasies are not unique to Ireland.

This case is of an Irish consultant obstetrician/gynaecologist carrying out 129 hysterectomies where, later, many were found to be unnecessary and/or without informed consent. Part of the public debate concerned the Catholic ethos on birth control and hysterectomies being used as a hidden form of birth control.

Dr Michael Neary was said to be well-intended but was, nevertheless, found to be in the wrong. He was eventually sanctioned for what happened. However, while Dr Neary was wrong, unfortunately, for both Dr Neary and his patients, he was allowed by his colleagues and nurses up to a point in time to continue with the non-consensual and unnecessary operations. After a complaint by a midwife to a Health Board solicitor about the number of hysterectomies, the matter became public. Nonetheless, the Irish Hospital Consultants Association asked three Irish consultant obstetricians and gynaecologists to examine nine cases. A report by the consultants subsequently exonerated Dr Neary. Unfortunately for the medical community at the time, there was a public outcry about the doctor's decision to exonerate Dr Neary.

We have here a useful case in point to help show that if the law of disclosure and informed consent was complied with, events probably would have been different. It would have been far better for all doctors and nurses involved, and the women who had their wombs removed. The story has dangerous implications for all specialities in medicine because the outcome surrounding the unnecessary hysterectomy operations could equally apply to other unnecessary medical or surgical procedures. One must think about unseating evidence and a failure to make disclosure and obtain informed consent and the duty of candour for adverse medical events.

Dr Michael Neary worked in the Our Lady of Lourdes Hospital, Drogheda. If the whistle-blower midwife was concerned about the hysterectomies that led to the inquiry, the publicity was indicative that others in the hospital over 25 years should have made it their business to find out if the patients were giving valid informed consents.[101]

If the law of informed consent was complied with, Dr Michael Neary, who was liked and respected by many patients and staff, is likely to have continued working in an approved way if his colleagues had intervened earlier. The whole truth of the Dr Neary case may help advance the important role of the law of disclosure and of informed consent, because it gives power to every level of professional carer involved, including the nurses in

---

[101] The Lourdes Hospital Inquiry, 'An Inquiry Into Peripartum Hysterectomy At Our Lady Of Lourdes Hospital', Drogheda Report Of Judge Maureen Harding Clark S.C., (2006). Available online at: https://www.gov.ie/pdf/?file=https://assets.gov.ie/11422/febc70aebb7840bb8bb65a4f6edbefcc.pdf#page=1

this type of complex situation to do and say something. If the female patients were told by any one of the professionals about the medical procedure in a balanced way as required by law, they likely would not have agreed to the surgery.

Another issue about disclosure in the Dr Neary case is that some of the victims took legal cases but were dismissed in the Irish High Court on the basis of the interpretation at the time of the Statute of Limitations laws. Based on the *O'Sullivan v Ireland* case (2019) in the Irish Supreme Court, these cases in the High Court may have been wrongly decided. Depending on the facts, the problem for the staff and management is that it may be still possible for victims to sue successfully.[102]

Nonetheless, some of the medical issues were complex about the need for hysterectomies on each occasion. Just because a woman had a hysterectomy, this is not an event that caused the time clock in the Statute of Limitations law to start.

There is, however, little room to contest that these tragic and personal stories for all the women involved would not have happened if Dr Neary's medical colleagues and nurses had discussed the need for the operation before their own medical interventions with the patient as part of the procedure. If a professional assisting with the system in some way failed to enquire if the patient understood what was being done and gave valid informed consent, the question is: Is this type of incident happening with some other types of operations that are unnecessary?

On a practical basis, nurses may be the key to intervening as they may have more experience than junior doctors in training and have a unique relationship with the patient. An anaesthetist or a nurse would be wise to protect themselves and enquire if the

---

[102] Oliver O'Sullivan v Ireland and others (May 2019)

patient understands the decisions they are making. Concerning Dr Neary's actions and those of the other professionals including the nurses, there is a lesson. One must consider in some future situations that a reasonable person in the patient's position may believe that the anaesthetist or nurse are in a vulnerable position legally and ethically. The anaesthetist and/or the nurse would be well advised to do as a judge must do and apply the reasonable person test as if in the patient's position. Ask: Are all the reasonable risks and reasonable treatment options disclosed and known?

**What Did the Anaesthetists Say?**

However, the anaesthetists told the judge in the Lourdes Hospital enquiry that they considered Dr Neary 'a safe pair of hands' and that 'they had never ever seen Dr Neary doing anything untoward in theatre'. The veracity of this evidence is absolutely not on inquiry here, however it's a useful reminder for the medical community that in a trial, such statements by the anaesthetists can be challenged on cross-examination with impeachment or unseating evidence if it exists.

Without any cross-examination opportunity in the enquiry, the Catholic nuns in the Lourdes Hospital said that they 'carried out orders and did not question consultants'. This, of course, occurred until the whistle-blower midwife exposed the events in the hospital. The Catholic nuns however were not following a nurse's obligations under the law of disclosure and informed consent, as the patients have a legal right to balanced information. If there is a differing opinion in the medical team, this is part of the appropriate information that must be disclosed prior to any treatment intervention to prevent an invalid informed consent from occurring.

Further and obviously, the law does not allow improper collegiality whereby there is an implied or understood agreement in the hospital setting between the medical staff not to contradict or be inconsistent with the senior doctor advising the patient about the medical options. On the contrary, professionals, including nurses, are obliged to give their independent opinion on the reasonable treatment options and obtain a valid informed consent before any intervention.

There were further problems, as three consultants who conducted the inquiry into Dr Neary were themselves the subject of an inquiry by the Irish Medical Council and were sanctioned for their conduct in arriving at this decision.

There was extensive media coverage quoting the judge who conducted the inquiry called the Lourdes Hospital Inquiry. Ms Eithne Donnellan, writing in the *Irish Times*, reported that Judge Maureen Harding Clark concluded that the three obstetricians 'have had serious regret for their part in producing these reports, which were motivated by compassion and collegiality'. Judge Harding Clark made reference to consent in her report and said, 'consent forms are too open-ended and do not have room for risks, benefits or alternative treatments'.

It's valuable to observe a pitfall, which is that Judge Harding Clark also said, 'Catholic nurses who were well trained knew their place, trusted the consultants and suspended their critical or questioning faculties'. A nurse is a professional person. Informed consent law equally applies to nurses and this suspension of a legal obligation is another problem or legal pitfall.[103]

In the same article, Ms Donnellan also told of an anaesthetist in the UK, Dr Stephan Bolsin, who had a bad experience after

[103]Ibid., The Lourdes Hospital Inquiry, (2006)

exposing the high death rates among children who underwent heart surgery at Bristol's Royal Infirmary. She wrote: 'Two surgeons there had mortality rates of more than 60 per cent when they performed corrective surgery on infants. Following an inquiry, new systems were put in place. But Dr Bolsin found it difficult to secure another job at the same level in Britain afterwards and left the country.'

To see the dangers and the benefits of this lesson, one must understand that things would have been different if there was a greater awareness of the law of disclosure: giving information and obtaining a valid informed consent, which is an ethical and legal requirement. This is where the interest in developing the law of informed consent lies. If valid consent was adequately adhered to in the case of Dr Neary, or the heart surgeons in Bristol, the patients probably would not have consented.

In considering the Dr Neary story, it's fundamental to the importance of the law of disclosure and informed consent to remember the obligations under the Convention for the Protection of Human Rights and Dignity of the Human and Article 5 on informed consent discussed in this book.[104]

### Example of Candour Published by the Health Service Executive

The patient's right to disclosure prior to a valid informed consent and the law relating to the duty of candour or open disclosure on medical errors is intertwined. It's possible for a victim's lawyer to claim that there is a legitimate expectation to be honestly and truthfully told of adverse events. In some cases, however, there has been an education problem where the

---

[104] Ibid., Article 5, https://rm.coe.int/168007cf98

medical community did not know they were making errors by failing to properly treat a patient after adverse events.

These medico-legal problems as they exist have been written about by Irish anaesthetists. The authors expressed a particular concern in Ireland about a deficiency in knowledge in the use of hyperbaric oxygenation. This deficiency in knowledge of a treatment option and the duty of making open disclosure about medical errors was brought out into the open by the professionals involved.

The Association of Anaesthetists of Great Britain & Ireland (AAGBI) in 2019 had 11,000 members, with approximately 4% from Ireland. A group of Irish consultant anaesthetists candidly wrote a report on what is a red flag medico-legal problem.

The report advocates that the medical community needs to be educated on the uses of hyperbaric oxygenation. In any event, their report is called the *Model of Care for Anaesthesiology Report for the National Clinical Programme for Anaesthesia* and was published to the Irish Health Service Executive. It was stated that patients are being deprived of hyperbaric oxygenation in certain circumstances, resulting in harm to the patient. At paragraph 11.4, page 77, the report states that: 'Patients have sustained iatrogenic cerebral artery gas embolism (CAGE) in Irish hospitals. Many of these cases relate to improper removal of central venous access catheters. Harm can be mitigated in these cases using recompression. These are avoidable events with devastating consequences for patients.'

Recompression here means using the hyperbaric chamber. The report also recommends 'that more should be done to educate the medical community'. The report's authors followed legal and ethical obligations as they made their concerns clear and informed the HSE about 'poor patient outcomes' and that 'the medico-legal aspect of delays to treatment for acutely injured patients needs to be considered'.[105] What is problematic for the medical community from the frankness of the *Model of Care for Anaesthesiology* report is, perhaps, the ignorance of the duties imposed by the law of informed consent issue of all those involved once they knew about an error.

From then on after the gas embolism, no further medical intervention can be made without disclosure, otherwise one obtains an invalid informed consent. The medical error must be disclosed. The patient has a legal right to decide to leave the hospital and take the rest of one's treatment elsewhere. A nurse, or any other medical professional, must say what happened. As was explained earlier, one cannot withhold the information that a mistake was made. This places strict obligations on all the medical professionals, including theatre nurses and all those taking part in the procedure.

The Health Service Executive in Ireland has been formally informed about these adverse events and the poor patient outcomes in the *Model of Care for Anaesthesiology* and is aware that medical professionals need to be educated. The Supreme Court has set out the duty of disclosure of adverse events in the *Ruth Morrissey v Ireland* case and others. At the time of writing, one does not know if those affected by the adverse events have been informed.

---

[105]National Clinic Programme for Anaesthesia, 'Model of Care for Anaesthesiology', available online at: https://www.hse.ie/eng/about/who/cspd/ncps/anaesthesia/moc/model-of-care-for-anaesthesiology.pdf

# Chapter Six:

# Uses for Hyperbaric Oxygenation

This chapter is about why and when hyperbaric oxygenation should be used. There are surprising legal pitfalls. There are medico-legal problems for medical professionals surrounding referral for hyperbaric oxygenation if they do not inform their patients about the known benefits. However, one will see the medico-legal problems of using 'lists' of indications. One must take reasonable care to explain to patients that they are entitled to more information outside any 'lists' about the use of hyperbaric oxygenation for their medical condition. One should not have a fear of being accused of quackery due to advising someone of a treatment option outside the box of standard care as, on the contrary, one has a legal obligation to take reasonable care to disclose the information. Acting based on a fear of being accused of quackery is not in the interest of the patient and is unethical. It's the same with refusing to give a letter of referral for hyperbaric oxygenation on the basis that one does not want to be seen to 'endorse' the treatment. This type of action or position taken could be the very cause of being successfully sued. It's legally problematic, as a victim's lawyer will use this doctor's position as artillery to show an invalid informed consent. This refusal to endorse could be interpreted as unlawful coercion of the patient to use the doctor's preferred treatment option. It could also be interpreted as unbalanced information or of unlawfully dissuading someone from using the treatment option.

Nonetheless, these lists cause the same legal problems for the medical professional as the editorial policy of the clinical practice guidelines discussed earlier. This is due to a failure of disclosure and to keep up with the changes in the interpretation of the law on disclosure and informed consent. One should consider what was said earlier about the Food and Drug Administration's misleading article called 'Don't be Misled', which was subsequently withdrawn. I believe that it transgressed against an obligation to give appropriate information under the European Convention of Human Rights mentioned earlier.[106] It was perhaps introvert of the US and it implied falsehoods that could have frightened someone off from using hyperbaric oxygenation, which was wrong. The article overlooked that, in Europe, free hyperbaric oxygenation is available for any medical indication under the European Cross-Border Directive if referred by a medical professional.

The 'Don't be Misled' article may be determined by a court to be a tort due to negligent misrepresentation and breach of a human right to adequate information.

---

[106] Ibid., Article 5: 'General rule: An intervention in the health field may only be carried out after the person concerned has given free and informed consent to it. This person shall beforehand be given appropriate information as to the purpose and nature of the intervention as well as on its consequences and risks. The person concerned may freely withdraw consent at any time.'

One of the two 2021 Overviews is an article published in the National Library of Medicine in August 2021 called, 'A General Overview on the Hyperbaric Oxygen Therapy: Applications, Mechanisms and Translational Opportunities'. It is useful because it sets out scientific applications for hyperbaric oxygenation.[107] However, the article gives a list of 14 indications, which is again introvert to the US's as it's the Food and Drug Administration's approved list. The reality is that outside the US there are more extensive lists as a result of broader clinical experience and a greater scientific focus.

Nevertheless, the article stated: 'Besides approved indications, further lines of research have demonstrated the potential applications and translation of HBOT in the field of inflammatory and systemic, conditions, cancer, COVID-19 and other conditions are summarized.' What is legally problematic is that the use of the words 'potential applications and translation' belies the fact that globally patients are using hyperbaric oxygenation for indications not on the list.

To protect against litigation, it's likely safer for the medical community in terms of the law of informed consent to set out scientific criteria for the applications. Because of legal reasons advanced in this book and the inconsistencies uncovered, a new way of thinking is required. As the law commands that a patient must be given an adequate explanation of the treatments, this must mean that the benefits and side effects of a particular drug must be compared with another drug, or with hyperbaric oxygenation, and this should be adequately explained. It must be legally beneficial to explain along the lines of the physical and biological phenomena of hyperbaric oxygenation on the one

---

[107] p. 864

hand, such as augmenting oxygen levels in the blood and tissue and the shortage of oxygen issues it can address.

Think along the lines of low arterial oxygen concentration or hypoxia tissue injury at a cellular level, inflammation, infection and/or diminished mitochondrial function. It cannot be said enough that it's a red flag issue to think ahead and see that this failure to use more scientific criteria is problematic for defending law cases, as this criterion is provable in an evidence matrix and is a wedge to open the door for compensation in litigation for victims.

Lawyers for victims can attack decisions made by the medical community by showing the contradictions and inconsistencies in lists of applications.

It's nonetheless important for the medical community to say it again: be aware of the tactics of victim's lawyers to unseat defence witnesses if they fail to give balanced information about hyperbaric oxygenation or nutrition or other reasonable treatment options.

The legal danger about the 'lists of indications' for uses for hyperbaric oxygenation is that victims' lawyers and expert witnesses can, with reasonable care, research medical journals in any speciality or in any country. They will Google and produce an article that discusses the application of hyperbaric oxygenation for the disease or medical indication. The two articles published in the 2021 Overview referenced here are an example.

The information in the *Medical Textbook of Hyperbaric Medicine* may be used. If one is a specialist in any medical field and hypoxic tissue injury at cellular level and inflammation are complications of the disease or injury, take a moment to Google-research the conditions of your speciality and hyperbaric oxygenation. In court or at an inquest, a judge or a member of the jury might be shown how easily this is done.

**Lists of Indications Causing Legal Problems**

Lists of uses for hyperbaric oxygenation created by medical associations, health authorities or insurance companies, or the equivalents of the Food and Drug Administration are legally problematic. To be clear from a legal perspective, in the US, the Food and Drug Administration only approves a list of medical indications, which in turn leads to insurance companies paying for the indications. Approval is not a disapproval of other indications.

What is dangerous is that if Dr X did not recommend hyperbaric oxygenation to a patient for a medical condition and gave a reason that the medical indication was not on a list of a medical society's recommendations, such as the Undersea Hyperbaric Medical Society, and Dr X thinks that one is safe from being sued successfully, in this case Dr X is wrong. It's the same danger caused by the clinical practice guidelines as, in a legal scenario, more disclosure is required, otherwise the medical intervention is based on an invalid informed consent.

In some countries such as the US, the list is not strictly based on science or even exclusively based on randomised controlled trials. Some indications on the list are based on clinical experience or historical use. Decompression illness and carbon monoxide poisoning were listed without randomised controlled trials. Still, lists are often used to simply set out the applications that insurance companies are paying for, for the treatment of customers.

In a European member state, in 2008, the Croatian national health authorities and the Croatian Institute for Health Insurance provided hyperbaric oxygenation as part of public and private cover to people in need of hyperbaric oxygenation for a newly extended list of indications. The list 'represents a compilation of accumulated international and national experience', said Dr Nadan Petri, of the University of Split.[108] The Croatian list includes the list of indications of the Undersea Hyperbaric Medical Society, the European Committee for Hyperbaric Medicine, including the latter's indications with lower-graded evidence and more indications recommended by other international or Croatian experts. In Croatia, like other countries, these indications are not considered 'off-label' as they are based on scientific reasoning and are part of standard care and paid for by the authorities.

The route to reducing cellular hypoxia, tissue injury, inflammation and infection is key. Like in other countries following this route, in Ireland, the Irish Health Service Executive's policy is to allow any public hospital consultant in any medical speciality to have independent discretion on what medical indication they use to recommend people for hyperbaric oxygenation, as the individual consultant sees fit, provided of course that the client agrees.

The Health Service Executive in Ireland has confirmed in writing in correspondence under the EU Cross-Border Healthcare Directive that there is no list of indications.[109] The Irish Health Service Executive has a National Hyperbaric Medicine Unit at the University Hospital Galway. There may be a waiting list for non-emergency use. Still, alternatively, people can be informed about free services in other EU states under the European Union

---

[108] Petri, Nadan, 'Hyperbaric medicine in Rijeka 25 years after the publication of the first Croatian list of indications for hyperbaric oxygenation', *Medicina Fluminensis*, Vol. 54, (2018), pp. 35-42

[109] In an email sent by the Irish Contact Officer under the EU Cross-Border Healthcare Directive.

Healthcare Cross-Border Directive or be told about private facilities.

A view of the law of informed consent is that it is refreshing and liberating for clinicians not to be confined to lists of recommended treatments. Importantly, it is in their financial interest to ensure they are well-informed on this issue.

Comments made by a medical professional on social media could be used by a victim's lawyer to unseat the defence's case.

Because of the global publicity about the jailed executives from Insys, the billion-dollar painkiller drug company, patients and the medical community have a growing hunger for variant treatment options to reduce the intake or eliminate the need for addictive opioids used as painkillers.

The first problem here for the medical professionals is that, in a legal scenario, it's the patient-centred approach that decides on the significance of the evidence. Nevertheless, as explained earlier, the victim's lawyer can show before and after PET or SPECT images, or inflammation blood markers from a textbook or medical journal.

The judge or jury will see the proof of hyperbaric oxygenation working. Because of the editorial policy of Cochrane Reviews, its meta-analysis often excludes what the reasonable person might consider significant. This is powerful unseating or impeachment evidence, and it's of value to know this now because this is what has already happened in courts regarding brain injury.

These are the new global legal problems being faced. Having explained the difficulty about lists of indications and the 'Don't be Misled' list, it will be useful to comment on a few indications by way of example that will help the medical community understand the law and the reasons for the needed explanations.

In 2021, two studies on the general application of hyperbaric oxygenation gave a useful overview of the type of information one's patient may need to be told. Nonetheless, both reviews would be improved if they helped medical professionals avoid litigation. The character of both studies is essentially setting out reasons why medical professionals might consider hyperbaric oxygenation a useful option. Nothing is said about the legal obligation on the medical professionals to give this information to their patients. To understand what might happen in a legal scenario, each drug currently being prescribed for an indication and their mechanisms of action should be compared with the mechanisms of action of hyperbaric oxygenation, along with the side effects of both. From a legal view, there is too much emphasis on non-scientific matters, such as the number of humans in the experiments. If you think this is wrong, I refer you back to the Harvard professor's comment 'about multiple consonant observations'. As a legal observation, authors seem to be unaware that many of the randomised controlled trials with a controlled group they reported on were probably unlawful and unethical. Interviews with the patients in the controlled groups about what was actually disclosed to them prior to consent is the measure as well as the already known benefits. The studies are referenced below and will be referred to the as 'the two 2021 Overviews'.[110] [111]

---

[110] Ibid., 'A General Overview on the Hyperbaric Oxygen Therapy: Applications, Mechanisms and Translational Opportunities', p. 864

[111] Ibid., 'Integrative Role of Hyperbaric Oxygen Therapy on Healthspan, Age-Related Vascular Cognitive Impairment, and Dementia' (2021)

## Neurological Dysfunction-Legal Dangers

Let's say that one is, for example, a neurologist being sued for failing to disclose that encephalopathy or a brain injury can be treated with hyperbaric oxygenation. Neurological dysfunction due to sports injuries will bring a lot of media attention to this area. There is a legal problem if a victim had a brain injury and the expert witness for the defence says there is 'no evidence' or 'poor evidence', and improperly dissuades the victim from using hyperbaric oxygenation or does not make good disclosure. The first problem here is that it's the patient and not the doctor who decides on the significance of the evidence.[112] Nevertheless, as explained earlier, the victim's lawyer can show before and after PET or SPECT images from a textbook or medical journal and inflammation blood markers. It's useful to say it again: the judge will see the proof of hyperbaric oxygenation working.

It's of pivotal importance for neurologists in a legal scenario to know that victims' lawyers will obtain other neurologists who will give evidence as to why their patients use hyperbaric oxygenation. Also, medical literature and witnesses can be used to show the known benefits. The problem for a lawyer defending a neurologist is that this evidence is available if a victim had a brain injury, concussion, decompression illness, dementia, coma, epilepsy, Parkinson's disease or other neurological disorders.

Nonetheless, surgeons embarking on brain surgery for trauma following an accident, or for Parkinson's disease for example, may not realise that they face further legal problems

---

[112] Rockswold, G.L., Ford, S.E., Anderson, D.C., Bergman, T.A. and Sherman, R.E., 'Results of a prospective randomized trial for treatment of severely brain-injured patients with hyperbaric oxygen', *Journal of Neurosurgery*, Vol. 76, No. 6, (1992), pp. 929-34

Zhong, X., Shan, A., Xu, J., Liang, J., Long, Y. and Du, B., 'Hyperbaric oxygen for severe traumatic brain injury: a randomized trial', *Journal of International Medical Research*, Vol. 48, No. 10, (2020), p.0300060520939824

because of the known benefits of oxygenation or hyperbaric oxygenation. As a neurologist, it's indispensable for clinical practice and avoiding legal problems to be aware of the extensive impeachment evidence in this area worldwide. Hyperbaric oxygenation is not new. What's new is the scrutiny of clinical practice in the information age, new technology to show benefits (evidence) combined with changes in the interpretation of the laws on disclosure in different countries.

To explain the artillery available to a victim's lawyer, it's helpful to see an example from Ireland of what could be used as unseating or impeachment evidence that a victim's lawyer can make use of to unseat a defence witness. It's likely to be similar in every country where hyperbaric oxygenation is available, nevertheless underused. It's similar to the case of *Brian Sponenburgh v Wayne County* in 1989, when the treating doctors failed to use the hospital's hyperbaric chamber and unfortunately from all sides paid out $3.08 million in compensation.[113]

The typical uses of the chamber in scientific terms could be considered by the reasonable person in the patient's position to be treating hypoxic (shortage of oxygen) tissue injury in the brain. What's legally problematic for medical insurers is that a victim's lawyer can prove this in a legal scenario by using circumstantial evidence, such as the emergency uses of hyperbaric oxygenation. Unfortunately, corrective action must be taken to avoid high-value insurance claims because hyperbaric oxygenation is underused in brain injuries, spinal injuries, sepsis or hypoxia at birth injuries, simply based on the law of disclosure and informed consent.

---

[113] Ibid., Sponenburgh v. Wayne County

If hyperbaric oxygenation is used by consultant anaesthesiologists in five neurological disorders in emergency medicine for hypoxic tissue injury, the logic is that it should be used by neurologists for other brain and nervous system tissue injuries. There lies the problem for the lawyers defending the consultant neurologists. As a neurologist, would one risk one's reputation and gamble that one's defence lawyer would successfully convince a judge that a reasonable person in the patient's position would not want to be told about hyperbaric oxygenation for healing tissue injury? This is the risk of losing law cases many may be taking. Concussion injury from sport will be the biggest problem area for the medical professionals because of the publicity.

The treatment of these emergency medicine conditions for tissue injury is paid for by the Irish Health Service Executive. These emergency neurological conditions are fundamentally hypoxic tissue injuries at cellular level, for example, stroke injury, radiation tissue injury in the brain, decompression illness, gas embolism and carbon monoxide poisoning. Lupus, which can become a neurological problem, is also treated.

Care must be taken by the medical community if making comments about information in this chapter. The medical professional may be conflicted or biased in a legal sense in the discussion, especially for a professional if one has not informed all of one's patients about the known benefits.

## A Barrier to Changing Concussion Guidelines in Sport

Unfortunately, what may be seen as a barrier to change in medical recommendations is an existing conflict of interest for the medical community. It's a case of taking the bull by the horns, for the experts involved. It's furthermore problematic for a defence lawyer, as a duty of candour is legally required of the medical professional where mistakes were made in past treatment given. Nevertheless, brain injury experts may fear that they will be 'damned if they do and damned if they don't' explain the known benefits of hyperbaric oxygenation for concussion. The problem is the existing artillery in the hands of the victim's lawyer. A defence witness will be cross-examined and asked to explain about the known benefits for hypoxic tissue injury in concussion and using hyperbaric oxygenation. In a legal scenario, there is a precedent that reasonable people in similar medical circumstances opted to use hyperbaric oxygenation since the 1970s and were given the information prior to informed consent to any medical intervention.

In simple terms, a concussion is a tissue injury in the brain. It's known that concussions can cause serious short-term and long-term medical problems.[114] In any case, hyperbaric oxygenation is shown in the medical literature to be extremely helpful. From a circumstantial evidence point of view, as already explained in a legal scenario, using before and after SPECT images of the brain, blood markers and traditional cognitive measurements, hyperbaric oxygenation is probably the most helpful and successful treatment option according to studies in many parts of the world.

The barrier discussed here that is preventing hyperbaric oxygenation from being used as a standard of care makes the controversy in the movie *Concussion* on Netflix, starring Will Smith as Dr Bennet Omalu, even more relevant. It's based on a true story involving controversial conflicts between neurologists. What did each side of the argument already

---

[114] Graham, N.S. and Sharp, D.J., 'Understanding neurodegeneration after traumatic brain injury: from mechanisms to clinical trials in dementia', *Journal of Neurology, Neurosurgery & Psychiatry*, Vol. 90, No. 11, (2019), pp. 1221-33

know about concussion tissue injury? The hero in the movie was Dr Omalu, a forensic pathologist, who in 2002 linked NFL players' concussion injuries to brain disorders called chronic traumatic encephalopathy (CTE) and behavioural mood problems in later life.[115] The tables eventually turned, and millions of dollars were paid in compensation to former players following settlements in law cases.

In a similar controversy with neurologists in the background, the author, publisher and TV journalist Tris Dixon tells in his book, *Damage, The Untold Story of Brain Trauma in Boxing*, that the brain damage was first called Punch Drunk Syndrome, then Dementia Pugilistica and then Chronic Traumatic Encephalopathy (CTE). Dixon's compelling story about boxing is an essential read for anyone who boxed or any doctor who treated boxers. It's told with clear-headedness and compassion, although traumatic brain injury in boxing is likely to cause legal problems for neurologists especially. Again, the research indicates that any boxer is facing an increased likelihood of early dementia. The major studies relied on by the Aviv Clinics from Tel Aviv prove the use of hyperbaric oxygenation.

The next stage is medical professionals being sued for failing to tell concussion patients of the dangers of not using hyperbaric oxygenation in emergency medicine. Patient's must be told about the inherent dangers of the delay factor in not using it. Nevertheless, there is still an opportunity to obtain benefit in using hyperbaric oxygenation even if delayed. We all understand the progression of a black eye getting worse in the days following the trauma. Further tissue injury occurs in the brain, such as with

---

[115] Laskas, Jeanne M., 'Bennet Omalu, Concussions, and the NFL: How One Doctor Changed Football Forever', *GQ*, (2009). Available online at: https://www.gq.com/story/nfl-players-brain-dementia-study-memory-concussions

concussion, and is similar to the inflammatory and tissue injury cycle of a black eye. Early emergency treatment is needed in concussion in similar fashion to the decompression illness or gas embolism.

Unfortunately, concussion is part of all sport, and life itself. Nevertheless, the discussion addressed here is about the treatment options for the injured tissue in the brain. A single concussion can lead to brain damage complications decades later. This is so, even if the person is diagnosed as having made a complete recovery requiring no further treatment.[116]

However, the medico-legal problems will be about a failure to make disclosure about the known benefits of hyperbaric oxygenation. This is where the law of informed consent becomes relevant and beneficial. It's a medico-legal problem for some consultant neurologists who failed to inform NFL players in the US and elsewhere, especially those dealing with rugby and boxing. The Netflix movie, *Concussion*, was about identifying the medical problem caused by concussions, but now this discussion is about inadequate concussion management guidelines in sport or in the rest of the community and why all patients are not told about the option of hyperbaric oxygenation.

The retired New Zealand international rugby player, Mr Carl Hayman (aged 41), announced in November 2021 that he was diagnosed with early-onset dementia and probable CTE, the degenerative brain condition. Unfortunately, in New Zealand, amidst a series of world-class rugby players who have suffered from brain and spinal injury playing rugby, some hospitals with hyperbaric medicine units still have similar misleading information on their websites like the Food and Drug Administration had.

---

[116] Ibid., 'Understanding neurodegeneration after traumatic brain injury: from mechanisms to clinical trials in dementia', pp. 1221-33

One will recall that the Food and Drug Administration in 2020 removed the misleading article called 'Don't be Misled'. It listed medical indications such as brain injury and other applications following the television exposure by journalist Duane Pohlman. I researched the websites of hospitals in New Zealand, Australia and other parts of the globe and found the 'Don't be Misled' list the Food and Drug Administration removed in 2020. I also noted that the Mayo Clinic removed a similar list from its website.

Mr Alix Popham, a former Welsh international, who in 2020 was also diagnosed with early-onset dementia, said he is using hyperbaric oxygenation. Dr Richard Neubauer (1924–2007), who had been reporting successful outcomes for brain tissue injury since the 1970s, has recommended up to 300 sessions depending on the severity of brain injury.[117]

In 2011, the NFL treated a player with hyperbaric oxygenation for traumatic brain injury and it's now a treatment of choice by players.[118] The NFL Super Bowl player, Mr Joe Namath, was interviewed in 2015 on Fox Business. He recounted how he used a hyperbaric chamber to treat concussion injury and stop dementia at an early age. Mr Namath did 120 sessions of this hyperbaric oxygenation for dementia and cerebral anomalies. Mr Namath, in the interests of all those suffering from dementia following concussion years earlier, generously published (for the benefit of all those in sport) the SPECT images of his brain that were taken every 40 sessions to monitor his progress.[119]

---

[117] Neubauer, R., Gottlieb, S. and Kagan, R., 'Enhancing 'idling' neurons', *The Lancet*, Vol. 335, No. 8688, (1990), p. 542

[118] Stoller KP., 'Hyperbaric oxygen therapy (1.5 ATA) in treating sports related TBI/CTE: Two case reports', *Medical Gas Research*, Vol. 1, (2011), p. 17

[119] Joe Namath on using a hyperbaric chamber to treat concussion affects. YouTube Fox Business. Available online at: https://www.youtube.com/watch?v=NPpOPRa4X0A

The *Concussion* movie and Mr Namath's interviews alone could be enough evidence for a judge or jury to determine that the reasonable person in the patient's position would want to be told about hyperbaric oxygenation for concussion as well as Alzheimer's disease, dementia and Parkinson's. It is likely that, in sport, concussion guidelines will be changed to include hyperbaric oxygenation as an essential treatment, however one may ask: How long does such a change take?

Again, suppose one thinks that one is safe from being sued because hyperbaric oxygenation is not 'the recommended' treatment in one's clinical practice guidelines, in this case one is wrong. If one thinks that it's a defence to say that hyperbaric oxygenation is not mainstream in a particular hospital or medical society, in these cases, one is wrong and not safe. The problem for a medical professional to overcome is that one must take reasonable care to become aware of the various treatment options in addition to the recommended treatment to enable good disclosure and informed consent.

No matter what area of medicine or surgery one practices, one must take reasonable care. Similar impeachment or unseating evidence likely exists in the country in which legal action may be taken. Nevertheless, even in Japan, Israel, China, Croatia and Egypt, where hyperbaric oxygenation is widely used, it is still underused and one can only speculate that this is because of a failure to make balanced disclosure.

With the cultural changes in a consumer society, extra care must be taken in brain injury and neurological dysfunction cases, as significant and sometimes rapid improvement or even remissions have been reported.

Suppose a victim's lawyer finds comments or tweets on social media from a clinician or one's medical society saying, 'there are no randomised controlled trials' or 'the trial has not been replicated' or 'I did not tell patients as I did not want to give false hope'. Or one might have said: 'Hyperbaric oxygenation was tried but it did not work [in circumstances where too few sessions were used for the condition]'. Even a medical professional saying to a patient, 'one needs to examine the evidence' without giving balanced information, could be misconstrued by the patient. A court could make a finding that the patient was not given balanced information and was in fact wrongly dissuaded from trying hyperbaric oxygenation.

Unfortunately, a victim's lawyer could call previous patients of the doctor being sued to give evidence of the quality of disclosure. Be forewarned that, in these circumstances, this evidence is likely to be used by a victim's lawyer to unseat or impeach the defence witness. Any decision not to give balanced information to a patient about a treatment option for fear of giving 'false hope' or wanting to 'control the patient's expectations', even if in the doctor's view it would be detrimental to the health of the patient, is no longer acceptable in a legal scenario for balanced disclosure and informed consent. Balanced information is key. One must tell the patient 'as it is' in a balanced way and not just give one's conclusion. This type of practice where the doctor makes the decision on the basis that the 'doctor knows best' is not lawful anymore. Nevertheless, what is legally problematic and something best to stop is a medical professional using negative unbalanced soundbites on social media.

It's a potentially problematic situation for the lawyers for the medical community when defending an invalid informed consent scenario. The actual language used by a clinician to deny culpability for inaction or to fail to make balanced disclosure about a variant treatment option could be used to strike down the legal defence. Clinicians are, as a result, advised not to use or tweet the coded language in medicine already mentioned.

Caution is wise as the meaning of 'standard of care' or saying a treatment is 'not recommended' is changing in the shrinking world, especially in the information age. It's valuable to be aware that using these coded terms or this language is problematic and often misleading or misunderstood in the eyes of a patient.

Nonetheless, the legal message here must not be lost. What the standard of care is in one's hospital or in one's part of the globe is not the test of what should be disclosed. To say that one did not tell the patient because it's not standard of care is circumstantial evidence that a victim's lawyer will use against a defendant.

As explained in other chapters, there is a problem if the defendant says that it was unreasonable for the doctor to know about hyperbaric oxygenation. The victim's lawyer can use a science textbook of a 12-year-old student explaining the universal gas laws to cross-examine a defence witness.

Nevertheless, the basic science is that applications for hyperbaric oxygenation are typically stated to be for treating 'hypoxic tissue injury at a cellular level' (oxygen want or cellular hypoxia) conditions. These applications are variously described as arterial insufficiency, ischemia, hypoxemia, tissue hypoxia, inflammation, neuroinflammation, and notably sepsis and infection. It's undisputed and well-accepted that hyperbaric oxygenation provides anti-inflammatory and anti-proinflammatory effects.

It's legally of value to know that surgeons frequently recommend hyperbaric oxygenation as near to surgery as is possible (especially elective surgery) and additional sessions as soon as possible afterwards. This is to bring extra oxygenation to tissue damaged during surgery.

These sessions are recommended, to speed up healing time of injuries, alleviate any need for opioid painkillers and reduce the possibility of infection.[120] [121] It's recommended in the Mayo Clinic for diabetic patients needing surgery.

On the opposite end of the spectrum, for failure to recommend hyperbaric oxygenation post-surgery, the medical community has been burdened with extra problems because of drug companies such as Insys, the opioid manufacturer referenced earlier.

### Fibromyalgia is a Neurological Disorder

In a legal scenario, imagine that every pain relief prescription or injection for fibromyalgia has been given with an invalid informed consent due to the failure to make balanced disclosure about hyperbaric oxygenation. An addiction to opioids could have been avoided.

For example, one of the opioid manufacturer Insys' addicted victims, Sarah, died because the level of opioids in her body eventually killed her. She worked as a nursing assistant but became addicted to opioids when prescribed them for fibromyalgia, neck and back injuries. On reading research from Tel Aviv on fibromyalgia, it emerged from the research that there was no need for opioids at all. Notwithstanding this history of opioid addiction and the culpability of the drug's manufacturers, compensation for unlawful death against the manufacturer in

---

[120] The Sports Surgery Clinic Santry and the Nuffield Health, Wessex Hospital, Southampton, UK are examples.

[121] Edwards, M.L., 'Hyperbaric oxygen therapy. Part 2: application in disease', *Journal of Veterinary Emergency and Critical Care*, Vol. 20, No. 3, (2010), pp. 289-97

these types of cases often becomes fruitless if the company becomes insolvent or files for administration.

So the question is: Who is on the list of defendants in different factual matrix scenarios? This is the legal problem facing doctors prescribing painkillers. The case of Sarah was reported in the *Financial Times*.

What's especially problematic for doctors with a patient addicted to opioids prescribed for fibromyalgia is the issue of informed consent and the various other treatment options.

Since a 2004 study from the Military Hospital in Istanbul, Turkey, a further study from Italy and several studies from Israel, hyperbaric oxygenation has been used for fibromyalgia.[122] [123] If one thinks that because it was not on the Food and Drug Administration approved list of conditions for payment, one is safe from litigation, again, in that case one is wrong. On the contrary, it's possible that the Food and Drug Administration will be joined as a joint defendant because of the 'Don't be Misled' list. Because fibromyalgia is a neurological disorder and is seen to be reversible in high percentages of cases with hyperbaric oxygenation, legal problems follow.

The recovery to that part of the brain with tissue injury due to fibromyalgia is observable with technology and, from the view of a victim's lawyer, is provable in a legal scenario. Impeachable evidence can be used by showing before and after SPECT brain images from various published clinical trials. It's further impeachment evidence that the treatment is being used by

---

[122] Italy. Muratore, M., Quarta, L., Puttini, P.S., Cosentino, C., Grimaldi, A. and Quarta, E., 'THU0512 Hyperbaric oxygen therapy (HBOT) treatment in fibromyalgia' (2018)

[123] Yildiz, Ş., Kiralp, M.Z., Akin, A., Keskin, I., Ay, H., Dursun, H. and Cimsit, M., 'A new treatment modality for fibromyalgia syndrome: hyperbaric oxygen therapy', *Journal of International Medical Research*, Vol. 32, No. 3, (2004), pp. 263-67

patients in the Aviv Clinics. But if the doctors fail to make good disclosure about the known benefits of hyperbaric oxygenation for fibromyalgia, that makes it a legal problem. Still, the danger passes to the prescribing doctors who may be successfully sued, depending on the case history. Aside from the obligation to give balanced information about the best evidence available, such as a study from Turkey, it's important from a legal perspective to know the accuracy of SPECT images showing fibromyalgia.

The victim can call evidence from radiologists and neurologists, who use a technique known as mapping, whereby they can identify the exact spot on the brain to look for hypoxic (lack of oxygen) tissue injury at a cellular level and cerebral anomalies.

Before leaving the discussion on fibromyalgia, in the 60-session study for a cohort of women with fibromyalgia who had a history of childhood sexual abuse, they each had to volunteer to come off all medication, including painkillers, and take part in the three continuous months of treatment for the study.[124] [125]

## Parkinson's Disease

A notable study in Russia on hyperbaric oxygenation and 64 patients suffering from Parkinson's disease of different aetiology dates back to 1989.[126] There exists a lot of impeachment evidence

---

[124] Hadanny et al., 'Hyperbaric Oxygen Therapy Can Induce Neuroplasticity and Significant Clinical Improvement in Patients Suffering From Fibromyalgia With a History of Childhood Sexual Abuse—Randomized Controlled Trial', (2018)

[125] Izquierdo-Alventosa R., Inglés M., Cortés-Amador S., Gimeno-Mallench L., Sempere-Rubio N., Chirivella J., Serra-Añó P., 'Comparative Study of the Effectiveness of a Low-Pressure Hyperbaric Oxygen Treatment and Physical Exercise in Women with Fibromyalgia: Randomized Clinical Trial', *Ther. Adv. Musculoskelet. Dis.*, (2020), 12:1759720X20930493. doi: 10.1177/1759720X20930493.

[126] VIa, N., Lobov, M.A., Kotov, S.V., Cheskidova, G.F. and Molchanova, G.S., 'Hyperbaric oxygenation in the complex treatment of Parkinson disease', *Zhurnal*

in the literature of the intervening period. In Japan, there was a study on rats with Parkinson's disease, where a lower dose of oxygenation was used in terms of pressure and percentage of oxygen (45%). Reasonable care must be taken that such balanced information is given to those suffering from Parkinson's disease, as the reports are extremely supportive, and I am witness to this in that I have seen people make dramatic progress.

**TNF Alpha (Immunosuppression Drug) or Hyperbaric Oxygenation?**

Humira, the pharmaceutical company, sold over $20 billion in 2021, so it's in popular demand and an interesting comparison with hyperbaric oxygenation. As a dangerous opening point from the patient's perspective, once the biological phenomena comparisons are explained by the doctor, any pharmaceutical TNF alpha immunosuppressants will be seen as commercial competitors and inferior. I said pharmaceutical, as hyperbaric oxygenation biological phenomena gets a better end result differently. Accept this position for a moment and understand that the danger for the medical community is that lawyers will latch on to the scientific evidence to prove the comparisons between the biological phenomena, whereas the unnecessary focus on the numbers of humans in randomised controlled trials as evidence will unfortunately be a losing factor.

In any discussion with clients, it's just as well to know that growing numbers in the medical community recommend hyperbaric oxygenation as a superior option to pharma immunosuppression or steroids in treating injured tissue and inflammation. In addition, hyperbaric oxygenation has an

---

*Nevropatologii i Psikhiatrii Imeni SS Korsakova*, Vol. 89, No.10, (Moscow, Russia: 1952), pp. 38-40

antimicrobial effect. In contrast, all pharma immunosuppressants such as Humira come with a warning that the medication can increase the risk of infection.

A further danger in medical practice is that if a medical professional prescribed drugs such as Humira or Stelara as a TNF alpha immunosuppressant, a judge or jury could determine that there was an invalid informed consent, because the comparative benefits of hyperbaric oxygenation and the drug were not disclosed. Patients on Humira are often on opioids as well so the difficulties of a defence lawyer are compounded.

The point is that one's patient could be on these drugs for years and then realise the lost opportunity for quality of life when they start using hyperbaric oxygenation.

In balanced comparisons, between using steroids or TNF alpha on the one hand and hyperbaric oxygenation on the other, it is collectively accepted, based on the universal gas laws, that the extra dissolved oxygen causes beneficial oxygen tension without immunosuppression. Hyperbaric oxygenation received attention during COVID-19 because it promotes a downregulation of proinflammatory cytokines (TNF-α, IL-6 and IL-10).

This superiority causes a legal problem for a defence lawyer if the difference in the mechanism of action is not explained adequately or at all to clients. In summary, technology can prove that this high-pressure oxygenation is a successful intervention to reverse hypoxic tissue injury, reduces inflammation and pain by healing tissue, and has the powerful antimicrobial effect. In terms of the law of informed consent, just because the Food and Drug Administration has approved Humira for nine indications and has not done so for hyperbaric oxygenation regarding all of those indications, this is not a defence for failing to make disclosure to patients that hyperbaric oxygenation could be used or at least tried for those same Humira indications. The inflammatory bowel disease issue discussed in Chapter Four is only one example of a comparison of treatment failure. An avoidable bowel removal is a high value claim.

**Heart Disease**

Firstly, people will want to know if hyperbaric oxygenation is beneficial for heart disease for scientific reasons, such as blood analysis of inflammation markers and endoscopic examination.[127] In addition, the law of disclosure and informed consent requires that the best available evidence at the time on heart disease be disclosed. The immediate obvious legal dilemma is, would a cardiologist gamble one's reputation and livelihood on the assumption that one's defence lawyer will successfully convince a judge or jury that a reasonable person with heart disease would *not* consider the following information significant?

In China, hyperbaric oxygenation is recommended for coronary atherosclerotic heart disease (angina and myocardial infarction). In 1992, the American Heart Association endorsed hyperbaric oxygenation for heart disease. In 2021, the American Heart Association part sponsored a major overview of hyperbaric oxygenation.[128]

In addition, part of the gamble is that, despite Cochrane Reviews' warnings of risk of bias and the need for caution, a victim's lawyer can nonetheless show that the authors stated, 'patients with acute coronary syndrome allocated to HBOT were associated with a reduction in the risk of death by around 42%'.

---

[127] Erythrocyte sedimentation rate (ESR), C-reactive protein (CRP) and plasma viscosity (PV) blood tests

[128] Balasubramanian, P., Delfavero, J., Nyul-Toth, A., Tarantini, A., Gulej, R. and Tarantini, S., 'Integrative Role of Hyperbaric Oxygen Therapy on Healthspan, Age-Related Vascular Cognitive Impairment, and Dementia', *Frontiers in Aging*, (2021), p. 49

Without going back over the chapter dealing with Cochrane Reviews and disclosure on medical laws, what was said about the issues surrounding randomising humans for trials and the 42% reduction in risk, the authors still say, without predicting what might be their patients' preferred treatment option that 'the routine application of HBOT to these patients cannot be justified from this review'.[129] One may understand from this position that neither patients' values nor the biological phenomena are not a determining factor, whereas it's the absence of quality randomised controlled trials that *is* the factor determining that hyperbaric oxygenation should not be routine.

If the authors are against the routine use based on the absence of quality randomised controlled trials and they have not disclosed this position to their own patients in their own practice, then in this case, they are biased in a legal sense and conflicted.

As regards statements about bias and caution needed, Cochrane Reviews failed to explain that randomised controlled trials should not be legally and ethically allowed to proceed. The starting point for giving balanced information to a person with heart disease is that one of the measures of heart disease is inflammation in the blood and plasma, and hyperbaric oxygenation reduces this inflammation in the blood and plasma. Simply put, this is the inflammation that causes hypoxic tissue damage at a cellular level, which in turn causes dysfunction. In layperson's terms, this is because hyperbaric oxygenation delivers oxygenation to the hypoxic injured tissue that is causing the inflammation. Again, the science supported by the universal gas laws is proof of this in a legal scenario. In terms of Cochrane

---

[129] Bennett, M.H., Lehm, J.P. and Jepson, N., 'Hyperbaric oxygen therapy for acute coronary syndrome', *Cochrane Database of Systematic Reviews*, Vol. 7, (2015)

Reviews helping medical professionals take reasonable care, they should give enough balanced information to help the medical professional practice within the law.

This life-saving information is not new, and this is problematic for lawyers defending the interest of clinicians.

Hyperbaric oxygenation is the treatment of choice for many people with heart disease and those at risk of developing it, when the known benefits are explained.

In simple terms, take a comparison of the biological phenomena of thinning the blood with drugs or using cholesterol suppression statins against information that hyperbaric oxygenation reduces inflammation by oxygenating and healing injured tissue. The latter is reported to have helped reverse the dysfunction of the injured or damaged vesicles transporting the blood, as it reduces the problematic inflammation and helps blood to pass through. Used over time, it is known to alleviate the need for a stent operation or open-heart surgery.

There is a legal problem for the defence lawyer if a patient dies of heart attack and the victim's family asks: Why didn't the doctor explain these known benefits? The known benefits in emergency medicine are that hyperbaric oxygenation as a treatment enhances the ability of clot-dissolving drugs to minimise heart injury and can save the lives of heart attack patients. What is the universal treatment if you were wheeled into an emergency centre with angina pain or a heart attack? It's generally accepted that you would be given an oxygen mask. In fact, the ambulance would also have given you oxygen. However, hyperbaric oxygenation is a higher or superior dose. If you have angina pectoris, hyperbaric oxygenation is used because you have suffocation of the heart that needs oxygen.

In the US, doctors have been advised by legal counsel to carefully note on each patient's file the conversation surrounding cholesterol-lowering medication, such as statin medication prescribed to prevent cardiovascular disease. There is litigation about statins and, again, care must be taken to give balanced information about the medical and legal controversy. Again, relying on clinical practice guidelines is problematic, as more information must be given apart from the standard recommended treatment options. Hyperbaric oxygenation is used in emergency medicine for treating stroke patients discussed in both 2021 Overview studies.

**Helping to Avoid Suicide**

We saw earlier how the TreatNow organisation was formed specially to help prevent suicide among army veterans by providing hyperbaric oxygenation. Laws can be problematic for medical professionals, because interpretation of the law at any one time can push out the boundaries. We saw how TreatNow is using the legal doctrine of the law of disclosure and informed consent to bring about a change in thinking.

It's beneficial for a clinician to consider the medical complications and legal problems of stress-induced inflammation. This inflammation causes tissue injury in the brain, which causes illness and disease. This cycle can lead to depression, then to suicide. Dr Daniel Amen, an American psychiatrist and author from Amen Clinics, says that, very often people who are treated by psychiatrists do not have a PET or SPECT scan of the brain to see if there is tissue injury as opposed to some mind disorder. He has illustrated a natural way to heal your brain without the need for toxic drugs.

All this can be problematic if treatment options are examined by the estate of the deceased person or a survivor who suffered an injury in the failed attempt at suicide. Suicide can be linked to tissue injury in the brain or some chronic medical conditions, such as chronic pain, headaches or opioid addiction. In any case, the choices of treatment options will be legally scrutinised. A similar suicide scenario can be triggered because of the poor quality of life with inflammatory bowel disease, herpes zoster, traumatic brain injury and related conditions. The existing evidence that is legally provable is problematic for lawyers defending clinicians. This is a reminder that randomised controlled trials are not required in a legal scenario when it comes to the law of balanced disclosure and informed consent.

### Matching Health-Span (period of healthy life) with Lifespan

Not being a burden is a powerful motivating factor for those using hyperbaric oxygenation as a medicine for dementia reversal and prevention. The unending love of mothers and fathers for their children is the major driving force. Money and time (three months doing 60 daily sessions) is invested because they don't want their dementia to become a daily strain on their children, grandchildren or partner. The bonus is the uplifting testimonials of those using hyperbaric oxygenation for brain health, and these are supported by observations using modern technology for analysing individual cells and SPECT scans of the brain. One can actually prove the reversal by observing the telomeres, cells that play a central role in cell fate and aging. This is why one can see that the Aviv Clinics in Florida and the Dubai programme, which included a 60-session cycle of hyperbaric oxygenation, will be the highly successful flagship leader. Everyone wants improved memory and cognitive function.

With the aim of having our health-span match our life span, hyperbaric oxygenation is used to prevent neurological dysfunction such as dementia, Alzheimer's disease, cognitive function, memory loss, balance issues, tremors and Parkinson's disease. Every person (100%) in these studies experienced an improvement. If hyperbaric oxygenation is used for healing, logically it can be used for prevention of the same disease.

The rationale of doing this 60-session cycle is that it heals injured tissue and reduces inflammation in all areas of the body. It further becomes a treatment of choice as a preventative measure against heart disease, eye disease, ear diseases, arthritic diseases, lung disease, stress and depression (inflammation issue again), bone disease, skin diseases and urology dysfunctions and more. It's a relaxing experience in a pressurised environment, so people may choose a lifetime of top-up once-a-week sessions.

## Infection

Because hyperbaric oxygenation is known as a potent concurrent treatment for the most serious of infections, it's used in the treatment of methicillin-resistant staphylococcus aureus or MRSA. This could cause medico-legal problems for the failure of not informing patients or their relatives of case fatalities before now. As a concurrent treatment, it has the same powerful and dramatic effect on infections, such as life-threatening sepsis, necrotising fasciitis, appendicitis (infected appendix), osteomyelitis (infection in the bone), encephalitis (an inflammation of the brain tissue), eye infections and more.[130]

**Pain**

There are many studies, however one of special interest is a study by sports medicine experts in the Hyperbaric Medical Center, Tokyo Medical and Dental University, which reports a reduction in swelling, pain and time of recovery. Again, it's because oxygenation rapidly reaches tissue injury and inflammation.[131] What is legally problematic is that medical professionals attending a sports event may unknowingly be breaking the law, especially when treating chronic injuries causing pain. This happens when injecting pain-killing medication because there is an invalid informed consent in place. This is due to the absence of disclosure on hyperbaric oxygenation. Emergency Medicine Departments in hospitals are exposed to the danger of being sued successfully if they don't make disclosure to patients of the availability of hyperbaric oxygenation either in their own hospital or elsewhere. Withholding information about the unavailability of a hyperbaric oxygenation unit so as not to upset a patient is now an unlawful reason, since the radical new interpretation of the law of disclosure in the UK in 2015.

Tissue injury and inflammation causes pain, whether in the brain or elsewhere. The two 2021 Overviews on hyperbaric oxygenation will be legally problematic if a medical professional

---

[130] Sanford N.E., Wilkinson J.E., Nguyen H., Diaz G., Wolcott R., 'Efficacy of Hyperbaric Oxygen Therapy in Bacterial Biofilm Eradication', *J. Wound Care*, Vol. 27, S20-S28, (2018), doi: 10.12968/jowc.2018.27.Sup1.S20.

[131] Yagishita, K., Oyaizu, T., Aizawa, J. and Enomoto, M., 'The effects of hyperbaric oxygen therapy on reduction of edema and pain in athletes with ankle sprain in the acute phase: A pilot study', *Sport Exerc Med Open Journal*, Vol 3, No.1, (2017), pp. 10-16

prescribes a painkiller without informing the patient about the benefits of hyperbaric oxygenation. Both Overviews deal with pain, chronic pain, joint pain, neuropathic pain, headaches and migraines. Investments in recovery from pain in sports injuries have led to studies on the subject. Any pharmacist will say that painkillers are one of the biggest over-the-counter products. A review of hyperbaric oxygenation on reduction of edema and pain in athletes with ankle sprain in the acute phase gives references to pain relief studies.[132] Balasubramanian et al. (2021) reference several studies on pain and hyperbaric oxygenation.[133] Studies on animals and humans have been positive.[134]

### Erectile Dysfunction, Prostatitis and Prostate Bladder Issues

Many studies have been carried out to correct arterial inefficiency and inflammation in other diseases, which show the benefits of hyperbaric oxygenation. It can induce angiogenesis in different body organs. For erectile dysfunction, several studies have taken place. One could read a useful study from Turkey and one from the Sagol Center in Israel which found similar successful results.[135] For erectile dysfunction following recovery after prostate surgery and post urethral reconstruction surgery there

---

[132] Ibid., Yagishita, 'The effects of hyperbaric oxygen therapy on reduction of edema and pain in athletes with ankle sprain in the acute phase: A pilot study', pp. 10-16.

[133] Ibid., 'Integrative Role of Hyperbaric Oxygen Therapy on Healthspan, Age-Related Vascular Cognitive Impairment, and Dementia', p. 49

[134] Sutherland, A.M., Clarke, H.A., Katz, J. and Katznelson, R., 'Hyperbaric oxygen therapy: a new treatment for chronic pain?', *Pain Practice*, Vol. 16, No. 5, (2016), pp. 620-28

[135] 'Sahin, M.O., Sen, V., Eser, E., Koc, E., Gumus, U., Karakuzu, C. and Ucer, O., 2018. The effect of hyperbaric oxygen therapy on erectile functions: a prospective clinical study. Urologia Internationalis, 101(2), pp.206-211.

are positive outcomes in studies.[136 137]

The Sagol Centre study is called, 'Hyperbaric oxygen can induce angiogenesis and recover erectile function'. They used state-of-the-art dynamic contrast-enhanced MRI (DCE-MRI) scans of the sexual organ to see before and after images of oxygen and blood flow reaching the penis. One should be aware that many MRI scans are out of date and newer models give better images. The MRI imaging was conducted using a 3 Tesla system (MAGNETOM Skyra, Siemens, Germany). These images are powerful and worth examining, as the increase in blood flow is seen. The images are published in the study. For sexual function assessment, they also used an International Index of Erectile Function (IIEF) questionnaire.

The 30 men who completed the study took 40 sessions of hyperbaric oxygenation at five sessions a week continuously over two months. The study only included men who had not undergone surgery in the pelvic area. The study showed that 80% reported positive outcomes. Before and after scores were given for sexual desire, intercourse satisfaction, orgasmic function, erectile function and overall satisfaction.

Erectile function improved by 88% according to the Clinical Efficiency Questionnaire. After the cycle of hyperbaric oxygenation, the study reported that 63% of the men had none to mild erectile dysfunction. The independent proof using the MRI imaging is reported as: 'MRI that showed a significant increase by 153.3 ± 43.2%

---

[136] Chiles K.A., Staff I., Johnson-Arbor K., Champagne A., McLaughlin T., Graydon R.J., 'A Double-Blind, Randomized Trial on the Efficacy and Safety of Hyperbaric Oxygenation Therapy in the Preservation of Erectile Function after Radical Prostatectomy', *J. Urol*, Vol. 199, (2018), pp. 805–11, doi: 10.1016/j.juro.2017.10.016.

[137] Yuan J.-B., Yang L.Y., Wang Y.H., Ding T., Chen T.D., Lu Q., 'Hyperbaric Oxygen Therapy for Recovery of Erectile Function after Posterior Urethral Reconstruction', *Int. Urol. Nephrol.*, (2016)

of K-trans v.'[138] As hyperbaric oxygenation induces generation of new blood vessels (angiogenesis), this brings increased blood flow to the area, which is objective proof as seen in the scans.

COVID-19 can cause erectile dysfunction. An interesting study found that cell dysfunction from COVID-19 infection can contribute to erectile dysfunction.[139] For the same scientific reasons for reversing hypoxic tissue injury at cellular level, hyperbaric oxygenation is significantly helpful.

## Prostatitis / Cystitis

It is suggested that the starting point in any discussion involving the bladder and the prostate is that hyperbaric oxygenation, in addition to reducing inflammation and infection, promotes rapid tissue repair and cell regeneration.

Again, because hyperbaric oxygenation for these conditions may have failed to pass meta-analysis and inclusion criteria for Cochrane Reviews or is not included in clinical practice guidelines, medical professionals have been under the wrong impression that they are not supposed to tell patients of it. On the contrary, they are expected to make disclosure to patients based on the law of informed consent. A reasonable person in the patient's position can expect as of right to be told that prostatitis, or inflammation of the prostate for example, is helped by hyperbaric oxygenation. Waiting for 'the flow' or having to get up at night

---

[138] Hadanny et al., 'Hyperbaric oxygen can induce angiogenesis and recover erectile function', (2018), available online at: https://www.nature.com/articles/s41443-018-0023-9.pdf

[139] Kresch, E., Achua, J., Saltzman, R., Khodamoradi, K., Arora, H., Ibrahim, E., Kryvenko, O.N., Almeida, V.W., Firdaus, F., Hare, J.M. and Ramasamy, R., 'COVID-19 endothelial dysfunction can cause erectile dysfunction: histopathological, immunohistochemical, and ultrastructural study of the human penis', *The World Journal of Men's Health*, Vol. 39, No. 3, (2021), p. 466

are the typical symptoms. Hyperbaric oxygenation is a patient's likely preferred treatment if they are informed, especially if they wish to avoid surgery.[140] Chronic prostatitis is one cause of male infertility and hyperbaric oxygenation is used for both prostatitis and fertility. Hyperbaric oxygenation chambers are built for racehorses. One of the most successful thoroughbred stud owners in the world, John Magnier, was one of the first in Europe to use hyperbaric oxygenation to help increase the fertility of both his mares and stallions. It's now also used to treat horses for illness and injury in the same way as humans.

**Cystectomy – Removal of the Urinary Bladder**

Regarding most diseases that are induced by hypoxic tissue injury and result in suggested surgery, the question is: Would the reasonable person in the patient's position like to be asked to try hyperbaric oxygenation as an option? Interstitial cystitis affects both men and women. Using hyperbaric oxygenation can save years of poor quality life. There is a randomised controlled trial from Germany however, even if there was no such trial, one must seriously consider what a patient would like to be told about hyperbaric oxygenation. Even without a case report, one should ask: 'Would you like to give it a try?' rather than a period spent in pain, loss of quality of life and being on medication treatments or facing a suggested cystectomy. As mentioned, there was a randomised controlled trial from Germany in 2006 using 30 sessions, but this is not the point regarding the law of disclosure

---

[140] HOBR – Hyperbaric Research and Development Centre in Lublin. https://hiperbarialublin.pl/en/benign-prostatic-hypertrophy/

and proceeding to treat someone with an invalid informed consent.[141]

## Transurethral Resection of the Prostate (TURP)

For the same reasons as healing tissue damage, again, hyperbaric oxygenation is likely a patient's preferred treatment if the patient is informed in a balanced way to avoid surgery. This discussion could continue. Using a cycle of 40 sessions has the added benefits of the effect on improved cognitive function, reducing inflammation in the joints or healing tissue injury, pain, or heart disease treatment or prevention.

## Simultaneously With Chemotherapy and Radiation Oncology

As stated, cancer is an emotional subject and one does not want any distractions from the message of this book. In addition to the chapter in the *Textbook on Hyperbaric Medicine* (sixth edition) and more recent studies in 2021, oncologists need to explain to their patients why hyperbaric oxygenation is being used to increase the effectiveness or potency of chemotherapy and radiation oncology.[142] The increased risk of not using it must be explained. Treatment programmes exist where radiation is given within one hour of hyperbaric oxygenation. Studies have

---

141 Van Ophoven, A., Rossbach, G., Pajonk, F. and Hertle, L., 'Safety and efficacy of hyperbaric oxygen therapy for the treatment of interstitial cystitis: a randomized, sham controlled, double-blind trial', *The Journal of Urology*, Vol. 176, No. 4, (2006), pp. 1442-46

142 Arpa, D., Parisi, E., Ghigi, G., Cortesi, A., Longobardi, P., Cenni, P., Pieri, M., Tontini, L., Neri, E., Micheletti, S. and Ghetti, F., 'Role of Hyperbaric Oxygenation Plus Hypofractionated Stereotactic Radiotherapy in Recurrent High-Grade Glioma', *Frontiers in Oncology*, Vol. 11, (2021), p. 964

and Alfouzan, A.F., 'Radiation therapy in head and neck cancer', *Saudi Medical Journal*, Vol. 42, No. 3, (2021), p. 247

shown that cancer strives in hypoxic conditions and oxygenation reverses this environment. The side effects of both chemotherapy and radiation oncology are reduced, such as tissue injury, loss of energy, pain or nausea. Certain types of chemotherapy are avoided so people can have hyperbaric oxygenation. In breast cancer treatments, it's used simultaneously with plastic surgery, post-plastic surgery in initial stages, and in breast reconstruction surgery to reduce risk of failure, period in pain and scar tissue.[143]

## Commercial Businesses for Reducing Stress

The spa and relaxation industry is growing. The medical community are trained to be scientific and want to see randomised controlled trials. Nonetheless, one must be careful about disparaging comments to patients about the role played by businesses promoting themselves as providing stress relief.

A spa or relaxation clinic offering a salt flotation bath could for example advertise on its website: 'our therapy is a natural, drug-free effective form of wellness therapy proven to balance your chemistry, neurology, physiology'.[144] A medical professional may be heard to say 'there is no evidence' but again this is coded language and should be avoided as it could be determined by a court to be non-scientific and the tort of negligent misrepresentation, especially if a patient is prescribed life-long medication for depression without disclosure on variant treatment options. Relieving stress and creating pleasurable

---

[143] Spruijt, N.E., Hoekstra, L.T., Wilmink, J. and Hoogbergen, M.M., 'Hyperbaric oxygen treatment for mastectomy flap ischaemia: A case series of 50 breasts', *Diving and Hyperbaric Medicine*, Vol. 51, No. 1, (2021), p. 2

[144] Salt, Floating and Recovery, Galway. More information available online here: https://saltfloatandrecovery.com/float-therapy-benefits/

experiences can help the body produce Serotonin. This natural chemical in the body plays a key role in such body functions as mood, sleep, digestion, nausea, and sexual desire. In this discussion, one must remember that a judge, as a fact finder, may determine from the patient's standpoint that there is sufficient evidence of benefits for one's mental and physical health.

**Lists of Indication**

Finally, it is with caution that one sets out these lists of indications below for the use of hyperbaric oxygenation in both China and Japan. There are two lists for emergency medicine and two for elective use. The reason for caution is that these are not the only indications. A medical professional will diagnose a medical condition and, if it's determined that hypoxemia and hypoxic tissue injury at a cellular level is the cause of the disease, one should tell the patient they might like to try hyperbaric oxygenation.

In the US, it's always safer to tell a patient that if hyperbaric oxygenation is not on a Food and Drug Administration list of conditions in the US, it could be because there were insufficient randomised controlled trials. As we have seen, the Nuremberg Code does not allow for random trials when the benefits of a treatment are known for a medical condition.

**Indications in China**

Every Grade A hospital in China must have a hyperbaric oxygenation chamber. According to Ling Yan et al, there are more than 5,000 hyperbaric chambers in China.[145] Hyperbaric oxygenation is commonly used on patients with ischemic hypoxic damage.

Emergency indications are diseases where HBOT should be administered as soon as possible. The following are emergency indications: (1) acute carbon monoxide poisoning and other harmful gas poisoning; (2) gas gangrene, tetanus and other anaerobic bacteria infections; (3) decompression sickness; (4) air embolism syndrome; (5) after cardiopulmonary resuscitation (CPR) due to a variety of risks for acute brain dysfunction; (6) aid in the treatment of shock; (7) brain edema; (8) pulmonary edema (except cardiac pulmonary edema); (9) crush syndrome; (10) limb (finger, toe) and the blood supply after skin transplantation; (11) drug and chemical poisoning; (12) acute ischemia anoxic encephalopathy.

Additionally, the following non-emergency indications are approved for use: (1) carbon monoxide poisoning or other toxic encephalopathy; (2) sudden deafness; (3) ischemic cerebrovascular disease (cerebral arteriosclerosis, transient ischemic attack, cerebral thrombosis, cerebral infarction); (4) craniocerebral injury (concussion, cerebral contusion of intracranial hematoma removal surgery, brain stem injury); (5) cerebral haemorrhage recovery; (6) poor healing fractures; (7) central serous retinal inflammation; (8) vegetative state; (9) plateau adaptation insufficiency syndrome; (10) peripheral nerve injury; (11) intracranial benign tumour surgery; (12) periodontal disease; (13) viral encephalitis; (14) facial paralysis; (15) osteomyelitis; (16) aseptic osteonecrosis; (17) cerebral palsy; (18) foetal developmental delays; (19) diabetes

---

[145] Yan, L., Liang, T. and Cheng, O., 'Hyperbaric oxygen therapy in China', *Medical Gas Research*, Vol. 5, No. 1, (2015), pp. 1-6

and diabetic foot; (20) coronary atherosclerotic heart disease (angina and myocardial infarction); (21) rapidity arrhythmia (atrial fibrillation, premature beat, tachycardia); (22) myocarditis; (23) peripheral vascular disease, vasculitis, e.g., Raynaud's deep vein thrombosis, etc.; (24) vertigo; (25) chronic skin ulcer (arterial blood supply obstacles, venous congestion, bedsore); (26) spinal cord injury; (27) peptic ulcer; (28) ulcerative colitis; (29) infectious hepatitis (use the special chamber of infectious disease); (30) burns; (31) frostbite; (32) plastic surgery; (33) skin grafting; (34) sports injuries; (35) radioactive damage (bone and soft tissue, cystitis, etc.); (36) malignant tumours (with radiotherapy or chemotherapy); (37) optic nerve injury; (38) fatigue syndrome; (39) angioneurotic headache; (40) pustular; (41) psoriasis; (42) pityriasis rosea; (43) multiple sclerosis; (44) acute Guillain-Barre syndrome; (45) recurrent oral ulcer; (46) paralytic ileus; (47) bronchial asthma; and (48) acute respiratory distress syndrome.

**Indications in Japan**

The application of hyperbaric oxygenation is covered by public medical insurance in Japan within the indications including:

1. Air gas embolism, DCI,
2. Carbon monoxide poisoning,
3. Severe soft tissue infection, including gas gangrene and necrotising soft tissue infections,
4. Intracranial abscess,
5. Severe thermal burn injury and
6. Frostbite,
7. Crush injuries and
8. Skeletal muscle-compartment syndromes,
9. Cerebral embolism,

10. Severe traumatic brain injury,
11. Consciousness disturbance or
12. Brain edema after craniotomy,
13. Severe hypoxic encephalopathy,
14. ileus,
15. Central retinal artery occlusion,
16. Idiopathic sudden sensorineural hearing loss,
17. Malignant tumour combined with radiation or chemotherapy, selected problem wounds and ulcer,
18. Skin graft,
19. Spinal nerve disorder,
20. Osteomyelitis, and
21. Late radiation injury.

**List on Mayo Clinic Website**

- Severe anaemia
- Brain abscess
- Bubbles of air in your blood vessels (arterial gas embolism)
- Burns
- Carbon monoxide poisoning
- Crushing injury
- Deafness (sudden)
- Decompression sickness
- Gangrene
- Infection of skin or bone that causes tissue death
- Nonhealing wounds, such as a diabetic foot ulcer
- Radiation injury
- Skin graft or skin flap at risk of tissue death
- Traumatic brain injury
- Vision loss, sudden and painless

**Approved indications published in Ortega et al. (2021)**

1. Air or gas embolism
2. Acute thermal burn injury
3. Carbon monoxide poisoning
4. Carbon monoxide poisoning complicated by cyanide poisoning
5. Central retinal artery occlusion
6. Clostridial myositis and myonecrosis (gas gangrene)
7. Compromised grafts and flaps
8. Crush injury, Compartment Syndrome and other acute traumatic ischemia
9. Decompression sickness
10. Delayed radiation injury (soft tissue and bony necrosis)
11. Enhancement of healing in selected problem wounds
12. Idiopathic sudden sensorineural hearing loss
13. Intracranial abscess
14. Necrotising soft tissue infections
15. Refractory osteomyelitis
16. Severe anaemia

# Chapter Seven

Returning to the Irish Republic, the epilogue to the Lourdes Hospital Enquiry on the unusual number of hysterectomies is valuable, as it helps all of us understand what can go wrong in any country in any hospital. The report noted: 'It must be understood that good, hardworking, decent people can unwittingly enable bad practice when support and safety systems are not in place.'[146]

My personal conclusion is that, globally, the legal and medical community as well as the courts have made mistakes in failing to support the right of the patient to be the decision-maker in medicine. Even the UK Supreme Court in 2015 admitted that its earlier decisions on disclosure were wrongly decided.

While in the UK the interpretation of law was changed overnight and was retrospective, it has been unfair and problematic for the medical community. A legacy is the culture in medicine that has been left behind. I speak of the unfortunate legal shortcomings of clinical practice guidelines that need to

---

[146] The Lourdes Hospital Inquiry, 'An Inquiry into Peripartum Hysterectomy At Our Lady Of Lourdes Hospital', Drogheda Report Of Judge Maureen Harding Clark S.C., (2006). Available online at: https://www.gov.ie/pdf/?file=https://assets.gov.ie/11422/febc70aebb7840bb8bb65a4f6edbefcc.pdf#page=1

change to help the medical community avoid invalid informed consents.

In the same way, the editors of Cochrane Reviews have a role to help the medical community to keep within the law. In this regard, almost an entire calling could be breaking the law on disclosure and ignorance of the law is not an excuse.

While a medical professional must take reasonable care to keep abreast of treatment options, this has not been the main problem or barrier to disclosure. The problem has been that these medical professionals who have been committed to their patient's interests did not properly understand their legal obligations to give balanced disclosure. Perhaps one had been reluctant about giving information on treatments options outside the box, in case one would be sued. However, many do not know that making balanced disclosure about this information is a legal obligation to obtain a valid informed consent.

Nonetheless, it took a law case about an invalid informed consent and a caesarean section as a medical option to radically change the interpretation of the law and medical practice in the UK.

In the US, it took a law case about carbon monoxide poisoning to make oxygenation and hyperbaric oxygenation the preferred treatment by patients.

A powerful support system to advance optimal opportunities in healthcare is to make sure that the patient is the decision-maker in every single medical intervention and only after full disclosure.

Is one's conclusion that a judge or jury will determine that a reasonable person in the patient's position with a traumatic brain injury would consider the known benefits of using hyperbaric oxygenation significant and that they should have been disclosed?

A judge is bound by law to make similar determinations on a range of applications for hyperbaric oxygenation based on the reasonable person test.

Is one's conclusion, like many in the medical community say, that many current standard of care interventions should be made redundant? Will doctors become redundant in certain specialities because current recommendations for treatments or surgeries will be rejected if patients opt for hyperbaric oxygenation?

The more seasoned doctors are adopting a new way of thinking, because they now approve of progressive doctors and of their patients agreeing to explore newer and potentially better medical interventions, relying on the best evidence available at the time.

It is likely that the temperature in the heated debate about nutrition in the medical community in the US will cool. Because of the law of informed consent, doctors from highly respected medical institutions will see that they can no longer refer to teams dealing with nutrition from other highly respected institutions as 'quacks'. Will they see that they will be creating circumstantial self-incriminating and unseating evidence against their own interest if they continue to make such claims of 'quackery'? This is because the patient decides, and all options and utterances must be looked at by the reasonable person in the patient's position.

Doctors should no longer fear being labelled as 'quacks' because their patients opt for something new where there are no randomised controlled trials.

Hyperbaric oxygenation only has a small role in healthcare compared to the potential and predicted impact that food, nutrition, fasting and lifestyle will make. Again, as Dr Mark Hyman said, 'food is not like medicine. It is medicine'.

## Value the Relationship

I believe that most patients will accept unreservedly the doctor's genuine apology for an oversight or mistake if it's properly made. The best apology, of course, is one without an excuse. Patients, by and large, greatly value their medical professionals. Mostly, they want to continue their special relationship with their doctors and value the out-of-the-ordinary service they provide, perhaps more than doctors know. What gives power to the special relationship between doctor and patients, is that the doctor explores the values of the patient and discloses the treatment options and the patient, at the end of the day, is the decision-maker, risks and all.

## Conflicted?

Nevertheless, great care must be taken to avoid a legal pitfall. Doctors or hospital managers may disagree with some of the points I have developed in this book, but before doing so, be aware that a victim's lawyer will seek to show how one may be conflicted. The usual declaration of no conflict of interest from the view of a victim's lawyer does not disclose any (vested) interest in protecting one's reputation for one's past errors or omissions.

However, there is a bigger vested interest that the medical community needs to be careful of. One may have a vested interest in protecting oneself from the possibility of being sued by a patient if a patient was deprived of balanced information on the known benefits of hyperbaric oxygenation.

Nonetheless, if a medical professional declares that there are 'no current competing interests', this doctor may be considered conflicted if they made calls for randomised controlled trials. Such trials may be considered unlawful and unethical in terms of the Nuremberg Code, the Helsinki Declaration or the European Convention, or unlawful in national laws in terms of the law on balanced disclosure and the law of informed consent, as I have suggested earlier in this book.

There is a need for medical professionals to seek independent legal counsel from their lawyers about the law of disclosure and the implications of an invalid informed consent. This is a need to be aware that the law applies to all levels of healthcare professionals.

Chapter Two of this book specifically addressed nurses, podiatrists, nutritional professionals, physiotherapists, speech therapists, dentists, physicians and surgeons. A nurse, for example, is recognised under the EU Cross-Border Healthcare Directive to refer a patient for hyperbaric oxygenation for wound care or other medical condition to an EU member state as it's paid for by the home state.

If disclosure was not made, one must take legal advice and stop using the legally problematic excuse of 'I did not want to give false hope'. While 'hope' in medicine is a complex subject, it also has an ordinary meaning and this position taken is not a defence for a failure to make balanced disclosure. Nevertheless, the use of the excuse about 'false hope' is likely to be used by victim's lawyers as artillery to unseat the credibility of the defence witness.

Nonetheless, care must be taken by doctors in this debate not to provide fresh unseating or impeachment evidence against the interest of the doctor when giving opinions or criticisms about the layperson's descriptions on the information disclosed in this book. In fact, each medical speciality needs to take reasonable care to update themselves on the law and treatment opportunities for their patients.

There may be an oversimplification, but in this debate, it is the best practice and is obligatory to always consider the reasonable person test and what the reasonable person in the patient's position would consider significant information.

## People Died of COVID-19

It's perceived by a cohort of doctors, hospital quality control managers, members of public and journalists that people died of COVID-19 unnecessarily. This is because of failings to use the best evidence available *at the time* and a systemic cultural failure to allow those suffering from disease or injury to make an informed medical decision and let the sick or injured accept responsibility for any medical risk.

The misplaced fear or worry for doctors of being blamed for making wrong medical decisions caused unnecessary deaths from COVID-19 and historically unnecessary or redundant medical interventions.

## Financial Institutions

The founder of Insys Therapeutics and six other executives were sentenced to prison for orchestrating a scheme to bribe practitioners to prescribe the opioid Subsys, a fentanyl-based pain medication, often when medically unnecessary. In a press statement issued by the US Department of Justice it said: 'Insys

Therapeutics executives profited by offering bribes and kickbacks in exchange for prescriptions of a highly addictive fentanyl spray.' [147]The drug maker also lied about how addictive the drug was.

In Wall Street fashion, it was short sellers in the US that helped bring about the bankruptcy of Insys. Short selling involves a method of buying or borrowing stock in such a way that if the price of the stock falls on the open market, one makes a profit. One by contract buys or borrows the shares at the lower cash price and one gives the shares back to the person they were borrowed from and the difference in price is the profit. Stockbrokers search for stocks they think will fall and profit if they do. In this case, the Financial Times story showed how the short sellers made the fall in price happen.

In June 2020, the Financial Times (London) published an investigative story about Insys called: 'Wall Street, bribery and an opioid epidemic: the inside story of a disgraced drug maker - Why were the warning signs around Insys ignored for so long? The FT and PBS series 'Frontline' investigate.' [148]

---

[147] Department of Justice U.S. Attorney's Office for immediate release.
Thursday, January 23, 2020. Available online at https://www.justice.gov/usao-ma/pr/founder-and-former-chairman-board-insys-therapeutics-sentenced-66-months-prison

148The Financial Times. Available online at
https://www.ft.com/content/eae603a4-a369-4801-a4cc-06232898a34f

The Financial Times told the story that 'Jim Carruthers, who runs his firm Sophos Capital from Silicon Valley, became suspicious because there were so few doctors prescribing so much Subsys. Carruthers had shorted healthcare companies before and began to piece together public data including which doctors Insys was paying, available under transparency laws, and the numbers of overdoses related to the drug.

He also hired a private investigator, who visited a top prescriber in Alabama, describing it as the "epitome of a pill mill'. After Carruthers set up his short position, he sent tips to journalists and the wrongdoing was exposed and the stock value fell, and a financial killing was made.

Because of this story, and the public interest in the press stories about doctors accepting bribes and kickbacks, accepting any gift or any (honorarium) payment from a pharmaceutical company is a particularly dangerous red flag area. Some pharmacies or drug stores have a computerised system of informing pharmaceutical companies the names of doctors who prescribed their drugs and the amounts. All of this is making inroads into disclosure (right to know) law and legitimate informed consent law. In a legal scenario, a court in the future is likely to find that a patient has a right to know if a doctor is being paid by the drug company to report on the effectiveness of a drug for example. What happened in the US eventually happens in Europe. It's therefore valuable to be aware of the impact of these financial institution's old tricks in shorting stock is bringing about new medical practice and changes on how doctors are traditionally encouraged to write prescriptions.

One is urging doctors in this book not to be complacent and to be more cautious. Don't be the first person in your city, state, or country to be charged with taking benefits that were considered normal practice that may be described in time as unlawful bribes. It may be considered a practice that a reasonable person in the patient's position would consider that should have been disclosed as part of obtaining a valid consent for the medical intervention.

The Financial Times article reported that: 'The company used tactics familiar in the US pharmaceutical industry - but took them across the line into illegality. Many drug makers pay speakers' fees to doctors, with the understanding that they will recommend their product to peers at educational events - but Insys made it clear that they expected more prescriptions in return for their money. Sometimes it abandoned the pretence of such events completely.' The article reported that: 'Seven of the Insys executives and employees on trial were found guilty of masterminding and participating in a scheme to bribe doctors to prescribe the drug.' Nevertheless, without knowing, a medical professional could have prescribed a drug to a journalist or private investigator who carried hidden cameras to prove a medical practice that could now be considered legally borderline.

However if the patient is not told about a payment for reporting on the drugs performance or is not told about a gift of a free flight and expenses to a medical conference, disclosure (right to know) law and informed consent law could be used by the short sellers to damage the drug company and stock price at the expense of the doctor's professional reputation.

**Targets on Stock Market**

A further question is: Will stockbrokers manipulate the market value of the shares of the manufacturers again and this time target immunosuppressants, blood thinners, statins or drugs for the treatment of cancer?

In conclusion, I should reiterate that Cochrane Reviews' authors and pharmaceutical manufacturers need to understand that, in medical experiments on humans, the patient must be absolutely central to decision making based on full disclosure. The patient must not be improperly used or abused.

The expression 'standard of care' is usually understood to mean treatments 'recommended' in the clinical practice guidelines. In reality, it's not a big change to say that the standard of care should include disclosure on the various treatment options.

The discussion in this book commenced with treatment opportunities for the global pandemic, COVID-19 and the law. One must hope that the lessons learned from the lost opportunities in treating COVID-19 patients and for other medical interventions discussed here have been a help to the medical community from a legal perspective.

Nothing further occurs.